Managing data wit

dBASE

Be an expert!

The *Be an expert!* series consists of books which enable you to teach yourself in an easy and straightforward way how to work with a computer program.

You simply follow the theory and the practical exercises and ... No trouble! It works!
This series aims at being both pleasant and educational.

Also published in this series:

- Programming with QBasic
- Word Processing with Word for Windows
- Word Processing with WordPerfect
- Designing with CorelDRAW
- Calculating with Lotus 1-2-3
- Working with DOS and Windows

Koos Mebius

Managing data with dBASE

Be an expert!

PRISMA

be an expert

Prisma *Be an expert!* first published in Great Britain by

Het Spectrum
P.O. Box 2996
London N5 2TA London

Translation: George Hall
Illustrations on pages 9, 14, 34, 55, 60, 67, 76, 78 & 134: Jurjen Tjallema
Production: LINE UP text productions

ISBN 1 85365 386 1

British Library Cataloguing-in-Publication Data.
A catalogue record for this book is available from the British Library.

Contents

The end of the Card-Index Age

Many ages have come and gone. There was the Stone Age in which everything was made of stone, the Bronze Age in which everything was made of bronze, even the clothes people wore. Those were the days.

Up until recently, we lived in the 'Card-Index Age'. Not because we really lived in card trays but because people made use of card-indexes to store information. Of course, this did not apply to **all** information; it applied to information which had to be quickly sought: facts about books (in the library catalogue), pupils' marks (in the school records), medical reports (in the doctor's filing cabinet) etc.

The beginning of the Database Age

Over the last few years, this kind of information has been stored in the computer instead of in the card tray. The card tray in the computer is not called a 'computer card tray', it is called a **database**. It follows that the program which organises the database is called a **database program**.

What is this book about?

One very well-known database program is **dBASE**. Many people nowadays work with version IV (thus 4) of this program. Version IV also has subversions. One of these is the modern subversion **2.0**. This book will deal with this version, dBASE IV 2.0.

We presume that this program is installed on the computer harddisk and that **none of the original settings have been altered**.

Please note that the pictures in this book have been made with a so-called **monochrome** screen. If you are working with a colour screen, everything will look just a little different. It may take a bit of getting used to, but you should have no difficulty with practice.

In this book, we presume that you know how to switch on the computer and that you possess the basic MS-DOS skills (how to save a file or create a directory).

Follow the fingers

The moving hand, having writ,
Goes on to write another bit.
This book deals with many topics, both in theory and in practice. Each time you have to actually **do** something, it will be indicated by means of a hand:

☞ Like this.

Even if you do not quite understand the procedure, if you simply carry out the instructions behind the hands you will get the correct result.

Tips

We shall also provide a number of handy tips in this book. These tips are displayed in a small frame with a TIP symbol:

T

Finally, we have to mention that dBASE is such an extensive, well-developed program that we cannot hope to deal in detail with all aspects within the scope of this book. That is not really necessary. If you can master the material in this book, you'll already be an expert!

1 Data management through the ages

Data, what's that?

It is a fact that this book exists. It is a fact that our alphabet consists of 26 letters. It is a fact that Paris is the capital of France. It is a fact that a person is 0 years old when born. It is a fact that a banana is bent. It is a fact that the current time is 10:15:23. I mean 10:15:24. I mean ...

These are all facts, pieces of data. One talks about data (mostly plural) as being facts, bundles of facts. You can save and store all kinds of data. But, as you saw with our last example, some data are only interesting at a given moment and later they are not interesting at all. In that case, it's of little use to try to store that kind of data. But it's a free world! If anyone wants to record the number of paces he/she makes every day, we have no objections.

Different kinds of data

You can divide data into certain groups. Names for instance, are data which are made up of **text**. The number of children that somebody has is a piece of data in **numeric** form. A birth date is a piece of data in **date** form. The fact that this book exists (instead of not existing) is a so-called **logical** piece of data: it is **true** that this book exists.

This kind of division into groups plays an important role in how data are stored and managed. For instance, you can do different things with numbers than with names. You can **add up numbers**, which you can't do with names. But you can **join names** together (first name and surname for example), which you can't do with numbers. We shall discuss this in more detail further on in this book.

Why should we manage data?

In the olden days, there weren't so many data. Take the cavemen for instance. They only went on holiday twice or thrice in their whole lives and they saved any interesting memories by drawing on the rocks. They could see what they had experienced by glancing quickly at the wall.

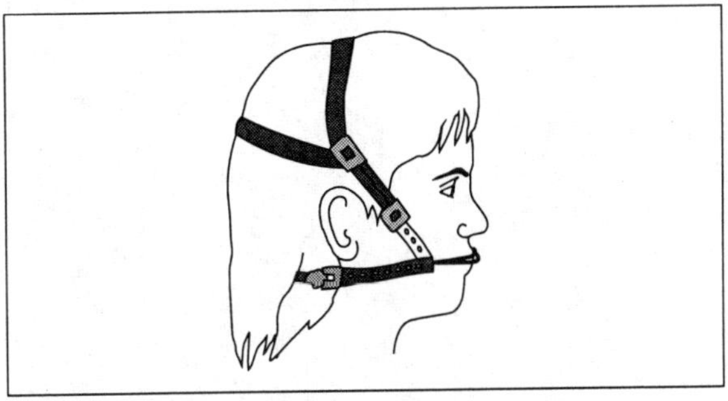

A caveman tries to keep hold of an interesting memory

But nowadays we have to have complete archives with photographs and negatives and video films to keep track of our holidays. If we want to have an extra copy of a photograph which was made at a particular campsite four summers ago, we have to begin an enormous search. In cases like this, it is very handy if the negatives have been stored in a good, logical, systematic manner. It is even better if we know exactly how to go right to the correct one.

This is the secret of good data management: **make sure that the data have been stored in an orderly way so that we can find the required pieces of data quickly and easily.**

Therefore: if there are more data available than required and if the required data have to be found quickly, a **good data management** is essential.

This is enough theory for now. Let's do something.

2 The Mammoth computer club

We shall create our first dBASE file. We shall create a file with names, addresses, telephone numbers and other information about the members of the Mammoth computer club in Keystone.

Getting organised

We shall first create a new directory and we shall then go to that directory. In this way, we make sure that the file we are about to create will be stored in the new directory.

- ☞ If necessary, switch on the computer. Make sure that the DOS prompt is shown on the screen (**C:\>** or something like it).
- ☞ Type **md practice** and press **Enter**.
- ☞ Type **cd practice** and press **Enter**. The prompt changes to **C:\PRACTICE>**. You are now in the PRACTICE directory.

Starting up dBASE

Now we can start up dBASE. That is very easily done.

- ☞ Type **dbase** and press **Enter**.

Note: if dBASE does not start up by means of this command, this will be because the computer does not know where to find the program. In that case, you should type the command **\dbase\dbase**.

The following screen appears after a couple of seconds:

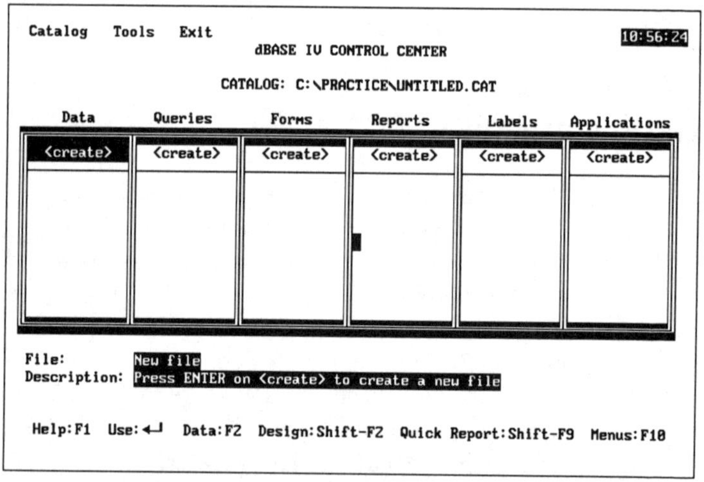

Depending on the settings in your dBASE program, the following screen might appear:

In that case, type the word **assist** behind the dot. Then press **Enter**. The screen which we are looking for then appears.

In the Control Center

What does this screen represent? On the second line from the top you will see:

```
DBASE IV CONTROL CENTER
```

This is thus the Control Center (American program, American spelling). You can run dBASE from here.

We shall discuss the various parts of the screen so that you can get an idea of what the program does.

The menu bar

Three words are shown in the upper left-hand corner:

```
Catalog   Tools   Exit
```

This is the so-called **menu bar**. You may be familiar with a menu bar from Windows or other similar program. This menu bar 'conceals' three menus: **Catalog, Tools** and **Exit**. How do you have a look at the menus? This is done by pressing the function key **F10**. Try it just for practice.

☞ Press **F10**. You see that the **Catalog** menu opens.

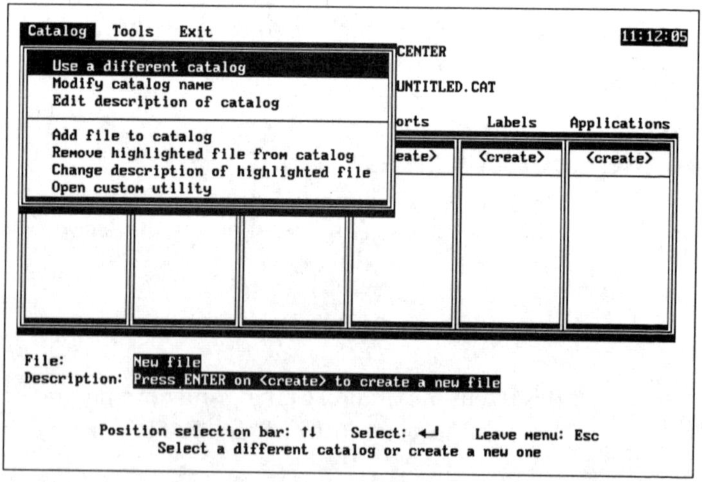

☞ Press the cursor keys as much as you want to move through the menu options. Don't be afraid, nothing can go wrong.

As you see, you can also move from one menu to the other. We shall not yet choose any of these options. In fact, we shall leave the menu bar again.

☞ Press the **Esc** key. We are back to where we began.

A built-in clock

As you will see, time does not stand still when you're at work in the Control Center. A clock is displayed in the upper right-hand corner.

The Help line and the F1 key

At the bottom of the screen there is a line which begins with:

```
Help:F1
```

This is the **Help line**, which means the line which provides help while you are working. The help information provided is usually very brief. For instance, at the right of this line you will see **Menus:F10**. This means that you can open the menu bar by pressing F10.

What is shown here depends on what you are doing in dBASE.

The **F1** key is very important in dBASE. It will provide information about what you are doing, regardless of where you are in the program. It will also provide other information about the program. We shall practise with this.

☞ Press the **F1** key. The following window appears on the screen:

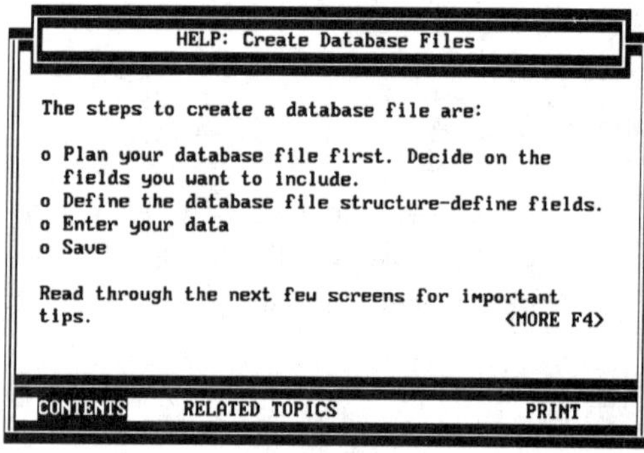

As you see, it really works: we want to create a file and that is exactly the topic we are given information about! How does dBASE know that? It is more straightforward than you might imagine. When you start up dBASE and have not done anything more, the program presumes that you want to begin by creating a new file. It is in fact a coincidence that we want to create a new file now.

Look at the Help line. It has changed. You are told that you can move to the next screen by pressing **F4** and to the previous screen using **F3**.

☞ Press **F4** twice and then **F3** twice to move back.

This indicates that there is more information about this topic than fits into one window.

You will see at the bottom of the Help window:

```
CONTENTS    RELATED TOPICS    BACKUP   PRINT
```

This is the Help window menu bar. The so-called marking is positioned on CONTENTS.

☞ Press **Enter**.

You are now presented with a kind of list of contents which deal with the creation and editing of files. If you examine the Help line, you will see that it has changed again.

☞ Press **F3**. You are now shown a list of **more general** topics.

We shall now leave the Help window for the moment and proceed with the explanation of the other parts of the screen.

☞ Press **Esc**. You can always quit any Help window in this way.

T ***Esc always lets you escape***

*The **Esc** key is always a saviour in need. If you are stuck anywhere you don't want to be in dBASE, just press Esc until you return to 'familiar ground'. You will often be asked this type of question: 'Are you sure you want to abandon operation?'. In such cases, answer **Yes**.*

Catalog?

The following sentence is displayed under 'DBASE IV CONTROL CENTER':

```
CATALOG: C:\PRACTICE\UNTITLED.CAT
```

You do not need to pay attention to this right now. This also applies to the two sentences above the Help line. We shall deal with them later.

The panels

The middle of the screen shows a window consisting of six **panels**. A panel indicates which files have already been created and which file is currently in use. There are various panels because you can not only have files with **data** in dBASE, you can also have files for printing labels, for instance. These panels enable you to have a good insight into the work you have carried out in dBASE. We shall only deal with 'normal' data files for the moment; thus, only the panel at the extreme left, **Data**, will be of use to us.

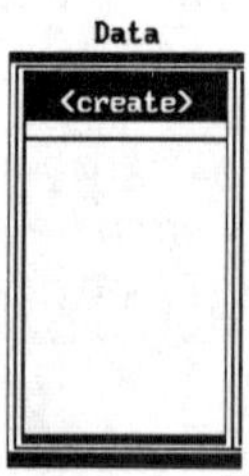

The mouse

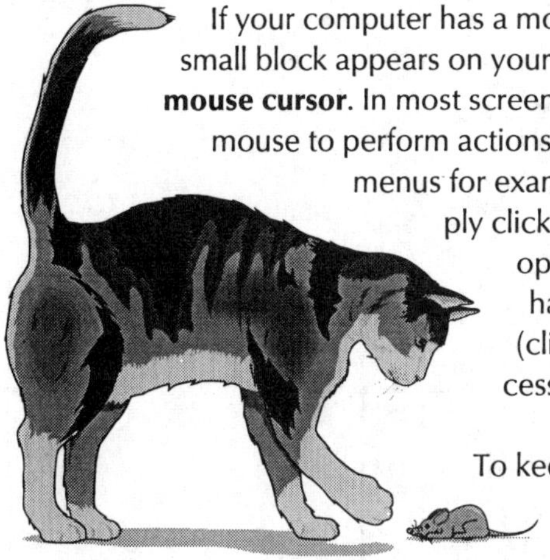

If your computer has a mouse, move it a little. A small block appears on your screen. This is the **mouse cursor**. In most screens you can use the mouse to perform actions, such as opening the menus for example. In that case, simply click on the required option. Sometimes you have to **double click** (click twice in rapid succession).

To keep this book as clear and simple as possible we shall not give instructions about how to use the mouse. In almost all cases, you can work just as quickly or even more quickly with the keyboard than with the mouse. Of course, you may use the mouse if you would rather do so. It's a matter of preference.

Now, finally, creating the file

You will see that the word **<create>** is displayed in a different colour in the **Data** panel. The word is **marked**. (If that is not so, move the ← cursor key to place the marking block on it.)

The Help line contains the following:

```
Use:
```

with an arrow with a vertical stripe behind the word. This means that if you press Enter, the file which is marked will be brought into **use**; it will be opened. But there is no file as yet and the marking is positioned on the word **<create>**. If you now press Enter, a file will be **created**.

☞ Press **Enter**.

A totally new screen appears:

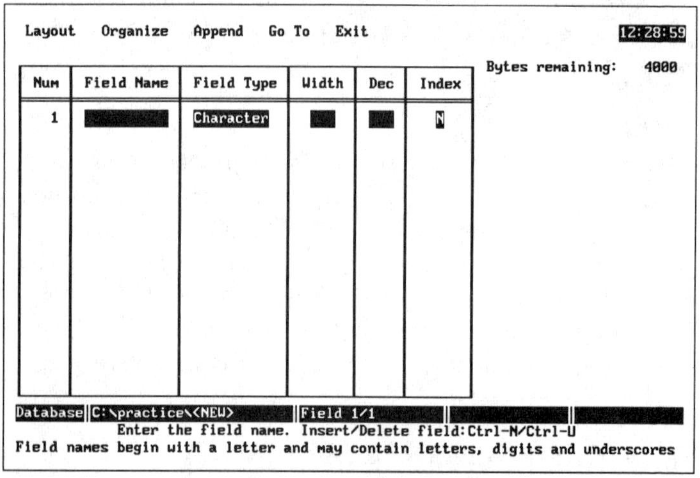

In this screen, you can tell dBASE how the **structure** of the new file is to be. We shall explain this in a little more detail:

Wood, bricks and steel?

We first have to think about the way the file has to be constructed, in other words, the **structure** of the file.

If you are working with a word processor such as WordPerfect for instance, it does not matter whether you write short or long sentences or type letters or numbers. Everything you type on the keyboard is adopted by WordPerfect. In principle thus, you can construct a file in an infinite number of ways. It makes no difference to the file: everything is accepted.

But dBASE files are a different kettle of fish. You cannot just 'dump' a load of data into a file. The data you enter have to fit into a certain **structure**, otherwise they cannot be entered. This has disadvantages but also benefits, as you will see.

You have to work out the **file structure** in advance. You can alter it to a certain extent later, but it is advisable to create it to your satisfaction right at the beginning.

A visit to the card-index tray

We discussed the card index at the beginning of the book. We shall now return to it for a moment.

How does a card-index tray work? Quite simply, as you probably know. It contains a number of cards which are all the same size. They are placed in a certain order of sequence, alphabetically for instance. Each card contains written or typed information: the data. If the card index is well-ordered, the same kind of data will be shown at the same place on each card. For instance:

Gates		2309
Name:	Gates, Bert	
Address:	386 System Drive; Procester PC1 2MS;	
Date of birth:	01-06-56	telephone: 01-111-222333
Notes:	was once a newspaper boy, now a millionaire!	

Of course it would be very confusing if the names were shown at different places on each card, for instance sometimes at the top left-hand corner, sometimes at the bottom right; it would make referring to them very difficult.

Each card has the same structure. There is a name, an address, a town, a postal code etc. Space is reserved for each of these pieces of data. For other data, such as somebody's weight, **no space** has been reserved. This is not considered relevant. You could perhaps place it under 'Notes' in special cases if you liked; but if there was no room for 'Notes' you would not be able to enter this information at all.

When we examine the cards, we see that the space reserved for the various kinds of data is not always the same. For instance, the Postal Code and the Date of Birth are short and don't need much space. The space behind them can be used for other data which are also not too long. The Name, Address and Town receive more space. Most is reserved for the Notes; this is a kind of box of cuttings - all kind of information can be stored here.

Thus, the structure of this kind of card has to take into account:

1. the **type of data** for which space has to be reserved
2. the **amount** of space reserved for each type of data.

One more word about the space. If you want to be able to store lots of data on each card, use bigger cards. But you have to make sure that **all** the cards are the same size. We can therefore add a third point to the two points above. The structure also concerns:

3. the size of the total space on each card (in other words, how big the cards are).

And back to dBASE

We shall now create the structure of the new file. This is comparable to choosing the size of the card and thinking about where the name should be placed and how much space should be reserved for it.

Records and fields

In dBASE we also work with a type of card. We call these cards **records**. The various kinds of data which we want to save on each card, thus in each record, are referred to as **fields**. Thus, there can be a field for the Name, a field for the Address, a field for the Postal Code etc. You determine the names of the fields which are to be used.

Each field has a particular length. In dBASE that is more precise than in a card index where you can enter pieces of information. In dBASE, you have to specify exactly how much space (thus how many letters or numbers) you want to reserve for a field. This is no problem for some fields. A postal code has no more than eight character spaces plus a space in the middle. A date of birth requires no more than ten. But a name or a town is different. You might be called 'Kok' like the Dutch Prime Minister, but you might also be called 'Boutros Boutros Ghalli' like the president of the United Nations or 'Her Royal Highness, the Duchess of York.'

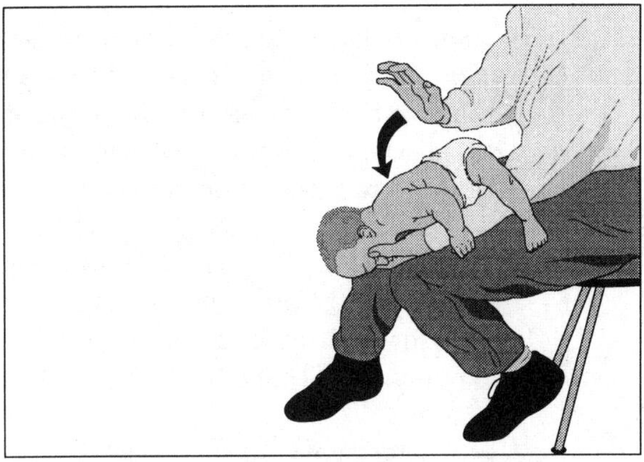

The youthful Duchess of York chokes on her porridge

Thus, you have to try to make an educated guess when specifying the length of some fields. You could say: if we leave an abundance of space, the name will always fit. But it's not quite so simple. If you use very long fields, they may not fit neatly onto the screen and you will quickly lose your overview of the 'card', which is certainly not our intention.

Do we still have plans?

Oh yes. Weren't we going to create a file? We shall first, however, give a short explanation of the various **kinds** of fields which can be used.

Various kinds of fields

In the introduction (The End of the Card-Index Age) we mentioned that there are various kinds of data;

there are data in numeric form, date form, text form and so on. These differences also mean that you can do different things with the data. For instance, you can work out how many days there are between two dates. You can't do that with names.

The dBASE program makes allowances for these different kinds of data. There are different kinds of fields in which these can be entered. The three most important filed type are:

- Character
- Numeric
- Date

The character field

You can place all the letters, numbers and other keyboard characters in a character field. This also applies to the characters produced by pressing key combinations using the Alt key, such as the **£** or the **é**. In a character field, the characters are only seen as characters. For example, a '4' is not regarded as being the **number** '4', it is seen as the character '4'. Therefore, you will not be able to add anything to this '4', just as you cannot add anything to an 'a'. A character field has a maximum length of 254 characters.

Examples of character fields are: a name, an address, a postal code (the numbers it contains are not used for making calculations), a telephone number (for the same reason) and so on.

Numeric field

A numeric field is specially designed for 'real' numbers, in other words, numbers which are used for calculation. If you want to create a field for the price of shoes or for the number of goals somebody scores in a season, you should create a numeric field.

In a numeric field, figures may also be placed behind the decimal point; you must specify this when you create the file structure. The decimal point is included in the length of the field.

Examples of numeric fields are: the membership contribution, the number of cigarettes a day somebody smokes, the number of children in a family and so on.

Date field

This should be obvious: this kind of field is specially used for dates. It always has a length of 8 characters. The century figures are never included. For example: **01-01-95**. As you see, dashes are placed between the day, month and the year. They are **not** included in the field length. You can also adjust dBASE so that colons (:) or slashes (/) are placed instead of dashes.

One of the advantages of a date field is that dBASE knows exactly which dates are acceptable. If for instance you try to enter the non-existent date **32-01-95**, dBASE will not accept it.

Enough is enough! I want to create the file!

If this is what you're thinking, you're quite right. Here we go.

It was a while ago, but your screen should still look like this:

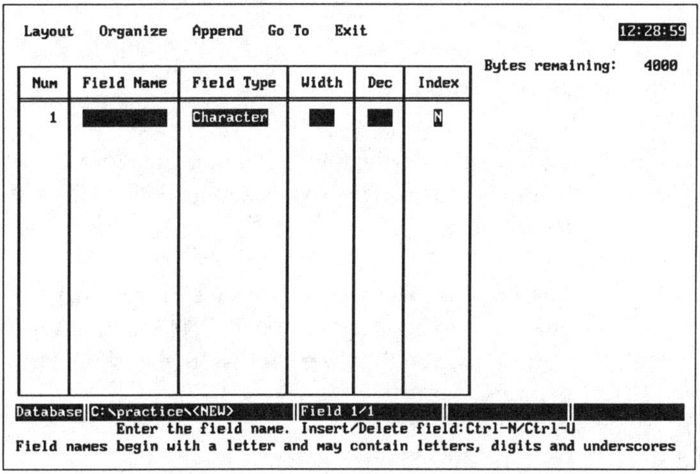

The Help line gives an indication of what you should do:

```
Enter the field name
```

The field with the 'basic data'

We shall begin with a field for the surname. We shall call this field **surname**.

☞ Type **surname**.

The name appears in the Field Name box, automatically converted to capitals.

Now press the Tab key to move to the third column. Here you can specify which type of field the SURNAME field is to be. dBASE suggests **Character**.

Of course, this is ideal for a name field so we shall not alter it.

☞ Press **Enter**.

Now it jumps to the fourth column. The word **Width** is shown at the top. We must define the **field length** here.

Yes, this is problematic. What is the longest name which has to be placed in the SURNAME field. We don't know yet. But if we specify 30, that should be enough.

☞ Type **30** and press **Enter**.

You see that the cursor skips the **Dec** column. 'Dec' stands for 'decimals' and it used to define the number of decimal places behind the point. Of course, this will not apply to a character field (ever heard of someone called 'Major.25'?).

The cursor is now located in the column under **Index**. We shall accept the setting as it now is.

☞ Press **Enter**.

You have now **defined** the entire first field. The cursor has now moved to the next line. We can now continue with the second field.

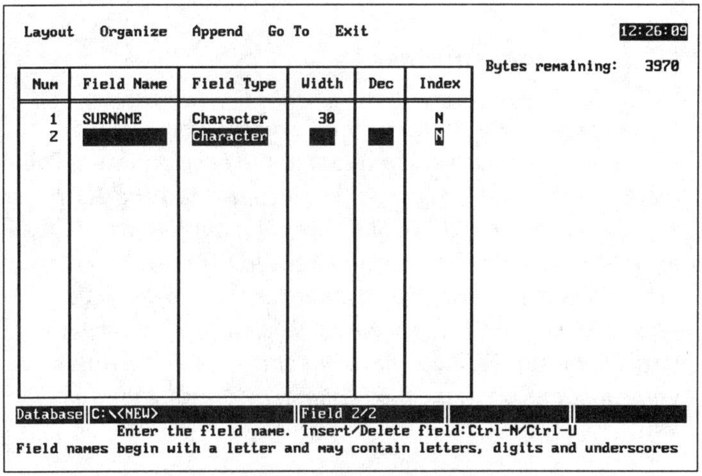

The second field will be used to store the first names. You could place the first names and the surnames in one field but it is more convenient to split these. You may wish to sort them alphabetically later.

☞ Type **firstname** and press **Enter** twice.

As you see, dBASE does not accept spaces in the field names. The Help line indicates that you can use letters, digits and underscores (underlining).

☞ Now type **15** for the field length and press **Enter** twice again.

Made a mistake?

*If you make a typing error, in the field name for instance, you can use various keys to return to the position where you made the mistake. You can for instance use **Tab** and **Shift-Tab** (press and hold down Shift, press Tab and release it again) to move on to the next or back to the previous column. Press the **cursor keys** to move through the letters. If you have not yet filled in a certain field, this will not always work. For example, if you have not entered a field name, you cannot move to the next column by pressing the Tab key.*

We can now begin on the third field. This will be the address. This too will be a character field.

☞ Type **address** and press **Enter** twice.
☞ Type **40** and press **Enter** twice.

The fourth field will be the town field. This of course is also a character field.

☞ Type **town** and press **Enter** twice.
☞ The width of this field should be **30**. Press **Enter** twice.

The fifth field is the field for the postal code. This field can only be a character field, even though it contains numbers. These numbers are not used for calculation purposes. In addition, this field contains letters and spaces.

☞ Type **postcode** and press **Enter** twice.

☞ Type **10** and press **Enter** twice.

The next field is to be the field for the telephone number. It's getting a little monotonous, but this field is also a character field. The numbers are not used for calculation purposes and in addition, there are dashes in the telephone number. Some telephone numbers can be really long (you might have cousins in Los Angeles or Sidney) so play safe: make this field **20** characters wide.

☞ Fill in the sixth field (**telephone**, **Character**, **20**).

The screen should now look like this:

Layout Organize Append Go To Exit 12:52:10

Bytes remaining: 3875

Num	Field Name	Field Type	Width	Dec	Index
1	SURNAME	Character	30		N
2	FIRSTNAME	Character	15		N
3	ADDRESS	Character	40		N
4	TOWN	Character	30		N
5	POSTCODE	Character	10		N
6	TELEPHONE	Character	20		N

Database C:\<NEW> Field 6/6

Enter the field width

Character fields are 1 to 254 positions wide

What other pieces of information are important in the club administration? Yes: the date of birth.

We shall enter this field as **birthdate** (otherwise the name is too long).

☞ Type **birthdate** and press **Enter**.

We have finally come to a field which will not be a character field. It is to be a date field.

The cursor is situated in the third column. Have a look at the Help line:

```
Change field type:Spacebar
```

☞ Press the spacebar.

The field type has now become **Numeric**. This is not what we require so continue further.

☞ Press the spacebar twice.

The field type has become **Date**. The length automatically becomes **8**.

☞ Press **Enter** twice.

And some extra fields

We have now defined fields for a number of 'basic data'. These fields enable us to register the names of the club members, where they live, what their telephone numbers are and how old they are. But it can be useful to store additional information. Accordingly, we shall create two more fields. We can add extra fields later if necessary.

The records are to be used for the members of the computer club, so we shall register the number of diskettes each member possesses. We shall also register whether or not each member has paid his/her monthly contribution. The amount of contribution depends on a number of factors and therefore is not the same for each member.

- ☞ Field 8 is to be called **diskettes**. Press **Enter** and press the spacebar once to change the type of field to **Numeric**.
- ☞ Press **Enter** and specify **3** as the field length. (The chance that anyone has more than 999 diskettes is rather small.)
- ☞ Press **Enter**. Half a diskette or a tenth of a diskette does not exist so we do not need to define anything in the Dec field.
- ☞ Press **Enter** twice.

Now the contribution field.

- ☞ Type **contrib** (the whole word does not fit), move to the Field Type column by pressing **Enter**, press the spacebar once and press **Enter** again.

Now we have to be alert. We presume that the monthly contribution will not be more than £99, so two numbers before the decimal point will be enough. There should also be two figures behind the decimal point, making a total of four. We must also include the decimal point in the total field length, therefore this field should have a length of **5**.

- ☞ Type **5** and press **Enter**. Then type **2** (for two decimal places) and press **Enter** twice.

Saving the file structure

We can now save this structure. This is done by means of the menu bar. You will have noticed that the menu in this screen is different to the one in the Control Center. We shall now activate the menu bar.

☞ Press **F10**.

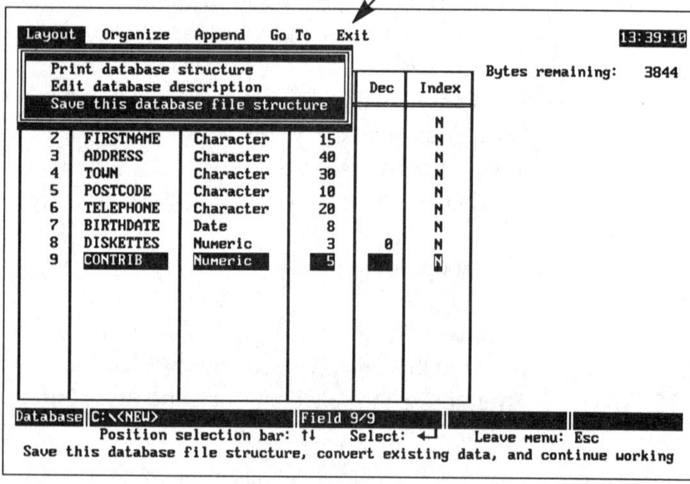

☞ Press the → cursor key to move to the **Exit** menu. Make sure the marking bar (the lighter coloured bar) is on the **Save changes and exit** option (it will probably already be situated there). Press **Enter**.

Now you have to specify a name for the file:

☞ Type **club** and press **Enter**.

You then return to the CONTROL CENTER. And what is shown in the **Data** panel? That's right, the word **CLUB**.

The marking bar is positioned on **CLUB** and the name of the file is also displayed behind the word 'File' under the panels. The letters DBF behind the file name indicate that the file is a data file in dBASE. dBASE places this extension automatically.

Closing down dBASE

We shall now quit dBASE. It is always useful to know this.

☞ Press **F10** and go to the **Exit** menu.
☞ Move the marking bar to **Quit to DOS** and press **Enter.**

Did something go wrong while quitting?

If you make the wrong choice in the **Exit** *menu ('Exit to dot prompt'), you will not move to DOS. Instead, you are presented with an almost empty screen. The status bar is displayed at the bottom. The cursor is flashing next to a dot. This is called the dot prompt. You can always enter commands here. Right now we want to close down dBASE, so type* **quit** *and press* **Enter**. *You then return to the MS-DOS prompt.*

You return to MS-DOS. You are still in the PRACTICE directory.

☞ Type dir **and press** Enter**.**

```
 *** END RUN   dBASE IV

C:\PRACTICE>dir

 Volume in drive C is GEORGE
 Volume Serial Number is 1B3B-11D8
 Directory of C:\PRACTICE

             <DIR>         30/09/94   10:28
..           <DIR>         30/09/94   10:28
CATALOG  CAT           439 03/10/94   14:04
UNTITLED CAT           258 30/09/94   10:31
CLUB     DBF           322 03/10/94   13:46
        5 file(s)        1,019 bytes
                   133,832,704 bytes free

C:\PRACTICE>
```

The CLUB.DBF file is listed in the PRACTICE directory. There are also two other files as you see. These have been created by dBASE. Pay no attention to these; ignore them.

3 Any data around anywhere?

We are now the proud possessors of an empty file, a file which only consists of a structure. We shall enter the data of the club members in this empty file.

Starting up dBASE again and opening the CLUB file

☞ Make sure you are in the PRACTICE directory. If C:\> is shown on your screen, type:

```
cd practice
```

☞ Now type **dbase** if you can start up the program from this directory or **\dbase\dbase** if not (see section 'Starting up dBASE' at the beginning of chapter 2).

☞ Press Enter.

After a few seconds the dBASE CONTROL CENTER appears on the screen. The **CLUB** file is shown in the **Data** panel:

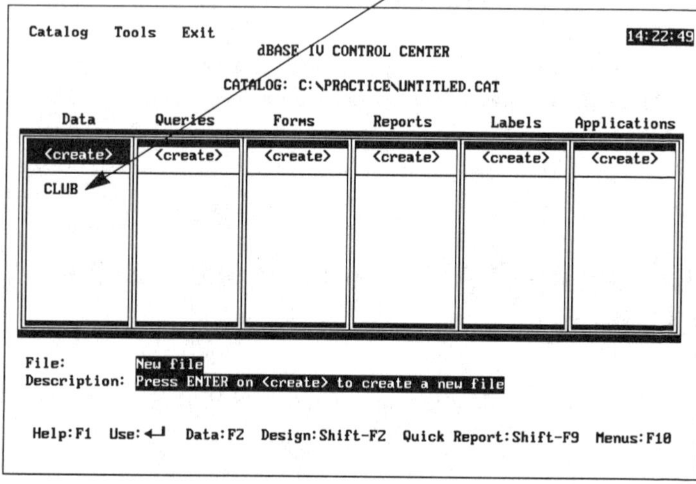

But do you notice anything special? The name is **under** the line. That means that the file is **not opened**. It is present but we cannot do anything with it yet. We first have to **open** it.

☞ Move the marking bar to the **CLUB** file using the ↓ cursor key and press **Enter**. You will already know that you can open a file in this way; the Help line also indicates this.

The following window is displayed:

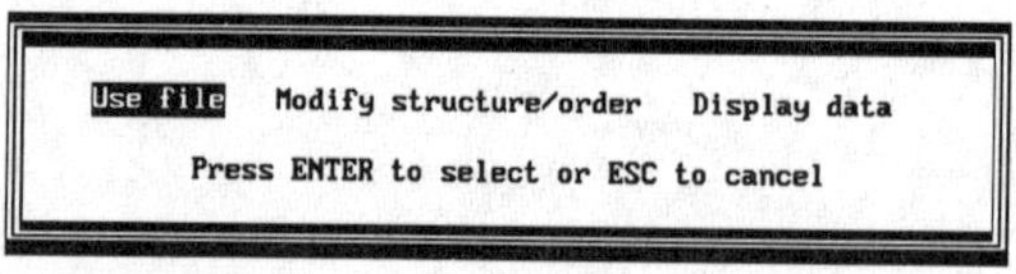

The marking in this file is on **Use file.** This is exactly what we want.

☞ Press **Enter.**

Entering the data

You will see that the file name is now shown **above** the line in the Data panel. This indicates that the file is **opened**. This normally means that the data are available and you can examine them. But there are no data as yet, so there is nothing to examine. We shall **enter** data instead.

Filling in the first record

Look at the Help line. The third item is:

```
Data: F2
```

Say no more.

☞ Press **F2.**

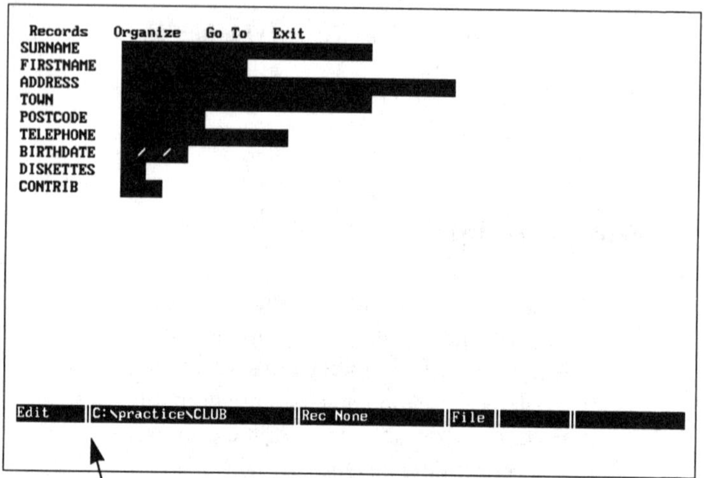

All the fields are shown in a list on the screen. The **status bar** is displayed at the bottom of the screen. It was also shown when you were busy creating the file structure. One part provides particularly useful information:

Normally the file name is shown and the number of the record with which you are working. There are no records as yet; that is why you see **Rec None.**

We shall create the first record.

☞ Type **Babbage** and press **Enter.** You can also press the ↓ cursor key.

The cursor moves on to the **FIRSTNAME** field.

☞ Type **Charles** and press **Enter.**

Complete the rest of the record using the following data (keep in mind that you can easily move through the record using the cursor keys if you have to correct anything):

```
1 Mill Lane
Loomington
LM1 1XT
07867-67431
14-05-82
15
7.50
```

Oh, oh? What's happened now? It seems as if the record has been deleted at the moment we typed '7.50'. But look closely at the status bar. You will see **EOF/1** behind 'Rec'. This means that there is one record and you are at the 'End of the File'. You are in fact busy with the second record!

It is easy to return to the previous record.

- ☞ Press **F10** to activate the menu bar.
- ☞ Move to the **Go To** menu and move the marking bar to **Top record.**
- ☞ Press **Enter.**

As you see, the previous record has returned.

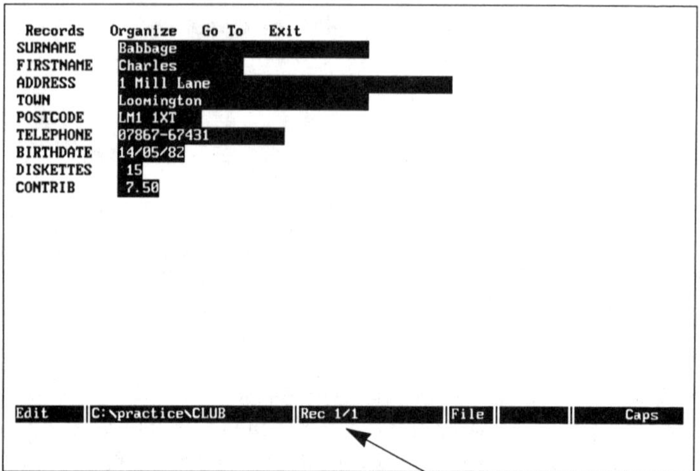

Look at the status bar. Its shows 'Rec 1/1'. That is true, you are at the first of 1 record(s).

Additional records

Of course, we have to create many more records since the club has many members. To add these records, we have to make use of the **Records** menu.

- ☞ Press **F10** and move to the **Records** menu.
- ☞ Select **Add new records.** In this rest of this book, when we talk about **selecting,** we mean: Place the marking bar on this option and press Enter.

The new empty record which was on the screen a moment ago, is restored. Fill in the following data:

```
Boole
George
21 Algebra Ave
Dublin
DB7 22P
00353-1-101-10101
18-12-82
20
10.00
```

The following empty record appears.

Continue with the following data:

```
Goldstine        Goldstine        Turing
Hermann          Adele            Alan
3 Eniac Cres     3 Eniac Cres     2 Enigma Rd
Washington       Washington       Manchester
WS3 5HP          WS3 5HP          MC4 2CD
0923-2525        0923-2525        061-888111
21-04-81         12-07-82         31-01-82
30               10               17
12.50            7.50             9.00
```

And then:

```
Lovelace         Stibitz          Weizenbaum
Ada              George           John
1 Byron Descent  1 Floating Pt    6 Eliza Gdns
London           Edinburgh        Liverpoool
L5 7WW           EH4 9TH          LV2 2EV
071-555-43221    031-431-2222     051-666-3333
03-11-81         11-10-82         18-02-81
12               27               11
7.50             15.00            7.50
```

And the last two:

```
von Neumann          Mauchly
John                 John
3 Edsac Edges        4 Whirlwind Prospects
Southampton          Ecclestone
SH2 7ED              EC1 1EC
0703-225-6161        0299-211-4567
18-05-82             01-02-81
17                   5
10.00                30.00
```

Browsing using PgUp and PgDn

*You can use the **PgUp** and **PgDn** keys to move quickly to the next or the previous record. This is an easy way of moving through the records to correct any typing mistakes for instance. Pressing **Ctrl-PgUp** will bring you to the first record and **Ctrl-PgDn** brings you to the last record. If you are at the last record and you press PgDn, dBASE will ask:*

*If you press **Y**, you can continue to enter new data.*

When you have entered the data concerning the tenth member, we shall save the file.

☞ Press **F10** and go to the **Exit** menu.

When the marking bar is positioned on the **Exit** option, the Help line shows:

```
Save changes to current record and exit
```

'Current' record means the record you are now working on. This would mean that this eleventh, empty record will be saved. Fortunately, the program does not work quite like this. If you stop now, only the other records are saved. But keep in mind, this is only the case if the eleventh record is completely **empty.**

The data in the other records are automatically saved when you move on to another record.

☞ Select Exit.

You now return to the Control Center.

Examining the data

As you see, the CLUB file is still opened; it is still above the line in the **Data** panel. Let's have a look to see if the data have been saved correctly.

The Help line shows 'Data:F2'.

☞ Press **F2**.

The last record appears on the screen.

☞ Press **F2** again and then **PgUp**.

As you see, the complete list of records is displayed on the screen:

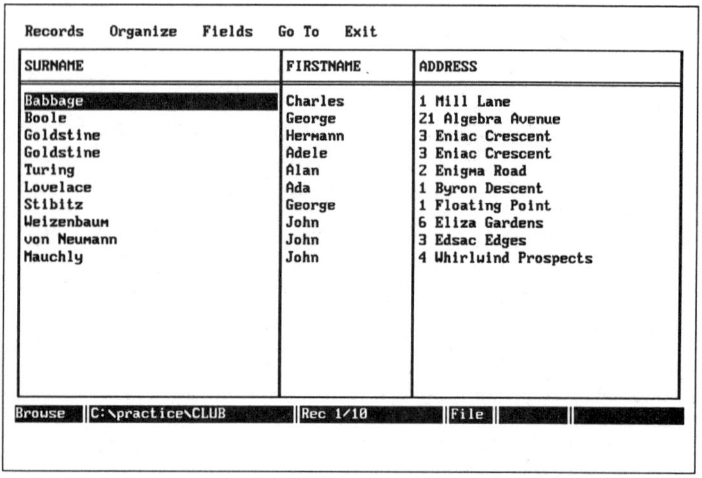

The records are listed under one another, one on each line. This is a good way to view them all at once; the only problem is that the screen is much too narrow: you can only see three fields.

Fortunately, you can also examine the other fields.

☞ Press the **Tab** key several times.

You will see that the list shifts to the left.

☞ Press five times on the ↓ cursor key.

The status line shows the **Rec 1/10** indication changing to **Rec 6/10**. The cursor is now in the sixth of the ten records.

☞ Now press **Shift-Tab** (Press and hold down Shift, press and release Tab).

The cursor moves across the screen in the other direction. In this way, you can **browse** through the records and fields. The word 'Browse' in the status bar (extreme left) also indicates this.

Leafing through the fields

The most important keys for browsing are:

Cursor →	to previous record
Cursor ↓	to next record
Tab or Return	to next field
Shift-Tab	to previous field
PgDn	to next screen (if more than 17 records)
PgUp	to previous screen (if more than 17 records)
Home	to beginning of the record
End	to the end of the record
Ctrl-PgDn	to the last record
Ctrl-PgUp	to the first record

You can also move back and forward within a record by pressing the ← and → cursor keys.

While you are browsing, you can also change, add and delete data. The **Del** and **Backspace** keys enable you to delete data.

You will gain a full overview of all the possibilities if you press **F1** and then **F4** several times. Try it out.

Changing data

We have heard from our members that some of the information in the records is not quite correct. We have to make some changes.

- ☞ In record 5, go to the POSTCODE field and change it to MC4 2C**L**.
- ☞ In record 9, go to the TELEPHONE field and change the area number to 22**4** instead of 225.
- ☞ In record 10, change the number of diskettes to **6**.

As you see, it's no trouble at all.

If you alter something in a certain record, the record is automatically saved **as soon as you move to another record**.

Switching to the complete record using F2

- ☞ Press **F2**.

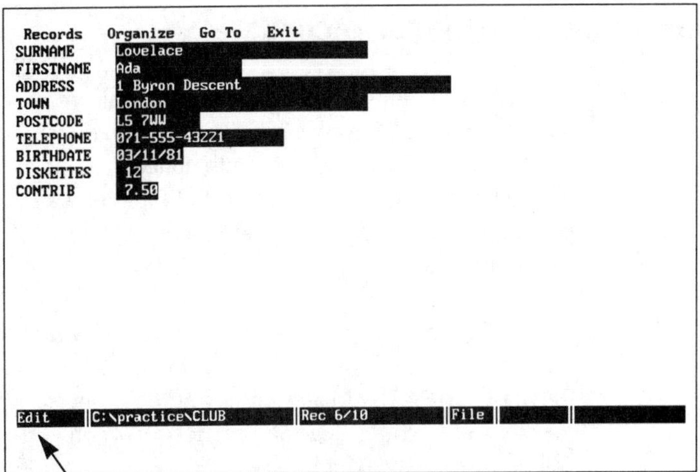

Here you see 'Edit' instead of Browse

Do you recognise this screen? It is the same screen as the one used to enter data. This is, thus, another way of examining data. The status bar does not show **Browse** this time, it shows **Edit**. While editing, you can move from one record to the other by means of the **Go To** menu, or by means of the **PgUp** or **PgDn** keys. **Ctrl-PgUp** brings you to the first record, **Ctrl-PgDn** brings you to the last record.

Data can be altered, added and deleted in this screen too.

The most convenient method of examining records depends on the kind of records you have. If you have large records with many fields, it is probably best to examine one record at a time. If you have small records, or if you only want to examine one or two fields in the records, it is probably handier to 'browse'.

Going to a particular record

We only have ten records, but lots of people who work with dBASE have many records, often hundreds, sometimes thousands. In that case, you would have to press PgUp or PgDn to move to a particular record. Or is there an easier way? Yes, fortunately there is.

We shall practise going to a particular record **without** having to make use of PgUp or PgDn (or Ctrl-PgUp or Ctrl-PgDn). In fact this is not really necessary for our file but it is good practice for when you will be working with larger files.

We are now at record number 6 and we want to go to record number 2.

☞ Press **F10** and open the **Go To** menu.
☞ Select **Record number**.

A small window appears:

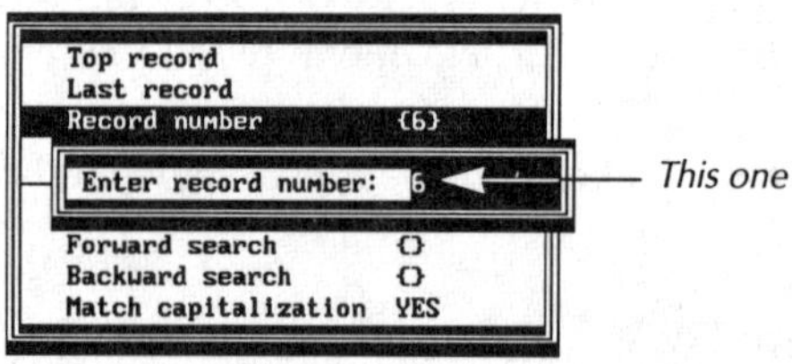

Number 6 is shown in this window.

☞ Press **Backspace** and type **2**. Then press **Enter**.

Record number 2 is displayed immediately on the screen:

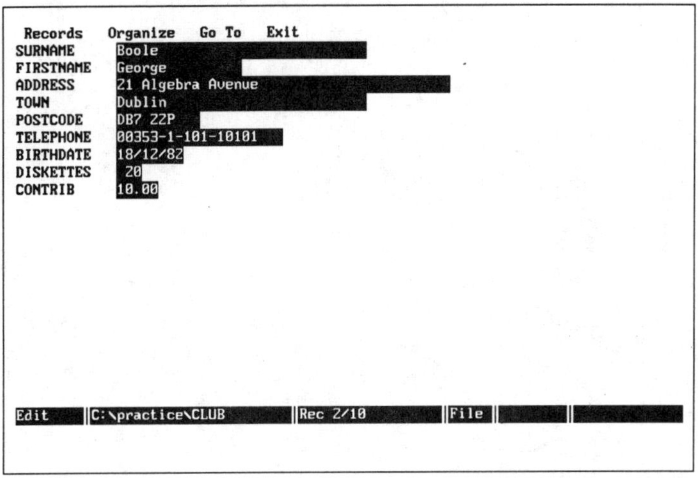

Searching

Of course, it is not always the case that you know exactly which record you want to go to when you are looking for certain information. What you often **do** know is a small piece of information: a name, an address or something like that. Sometimes you only know a **part** of a name.

Fortunately, dBASE makes it quite easy to search for certain data. That can be done in various ways. We shall now outline one of these ways.

We shall look for the record belonging to someone living in Ecclestone.

☞ Place the cursor in the **TOWN** field.
☞ Press **F10** and open the **Go To** menu.
☞ Select the **Forwards search** option.

A small window appears:

☞ Type **Ecclestone** and press **Enter**.

The required record (Mauchly from Ecclestone) appears on your screen.

You are now at record number 10, the last record. If you now want to search for another record, it will have to be in front of this record. Does this mean that you have to select **Backward search** for the next search command? No, that's not necessary. If dBASE reaches the end of the file while it is searching, it simply begins at the beginning of the file and continues until the entire file has been examined.

If you have a very large file, it might be cleverer to search backwards if you know that the record you are looking for is situated in front of the currently active record. In that case, the search will be less time-consuming.

The difference between capitals and small letters

We shall now look for a resident of London.

☞ Make sure the cursor is positioned in the **TOWN** field, press **F10** and open the **Go To** menu.
☞ Select the **Forward search** option.
☞ Type **london** (without a capital).

The following window appears:

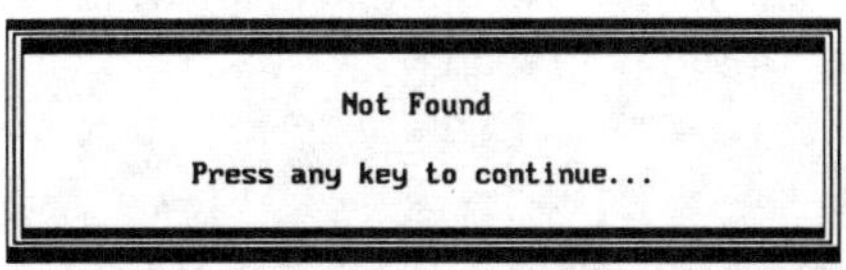

What's going on? This happens because the sought word is **not exactly the same** as the word in the record. You should have typed a capital **L**. We shall try again.

☞ Press any key.

- ☞ Select **Forward search** again and change the first letter to a capital.
- ☞ Press **Enter**.

This time you will be successful.

T

No difference between capitals and small letters if you want

*You can change the settings in dBASE so that when you are searching, no distinction will be made between capitals and small letters. To do this, open the **Go To** menu and select **Match capitalization**. Press **Enter**. The word **Yes** shown behind this option then changes to **NO**. This will remain the normal setting until you quit dBASE or change the option back to YES.*

All these actions can also be performed when you have the list of files displayed on the screen.

When searching, do not forget that the cursor should be placed in the field for which you are performing the search.

Saving a record when you don't go to another record

As you now know, each change to the data is saved when you move on to another record. Now try the following:

☞ Change George Boole's address in record 2 to number **22** Algebra Avenue.
☞ Press **Esc**.

You return to the Control Center. The file is still opened; it is still above the line. We shall now examine the data.

☞ Press **F2**.

You are immediately shown the contents of record 2 because the so-called **record pointer** was still positioned on this record and the file was still opened. Look at the address: it is still number **21**.

☞ Change the address to number **22** again.
☞ Press **Ctrl-End**.

You have returned to the Control Center; but this time the changes have been saved.

☞ Press **F2**.

You see that the change has been made permanent.

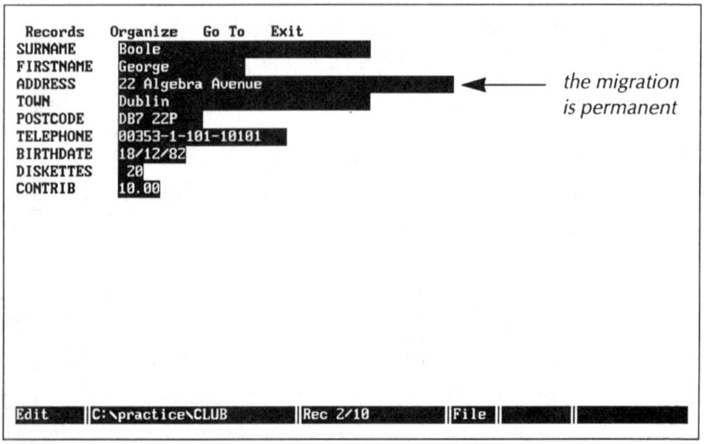

the migration is permanent

☞ Press **Esc**.

Changing the file structure

We shall make a few changes to the file structure. We have realised that it would be very useful if the members of the computer club were to have **membership numbers**. Therefore, we should create an additional field for the number. In addition, we have seen that the fields for the SURNAME, FIRSTNAME, ADDRESS and TOWN are rather long. This makes it difficult to get a good view of all the fields when browsing.

This often happens in practice. It is very sensible to think about the structure in advance, but sometimes you have to be prepared to change it later to fit the practical needs. Nevertheless, if you are going to shorten fields or even remove them altogether, pay close attention to what you're doing!

☞ Examine the Help line in the Control Center. You will see:

```
Design:Shift-F2
```

'Design' in this case is the same as 'structure'.

☞ Press **Shift-F2**.

The same screen appears as when you created the file structure. This time dBASE also opens a menu at the same time.

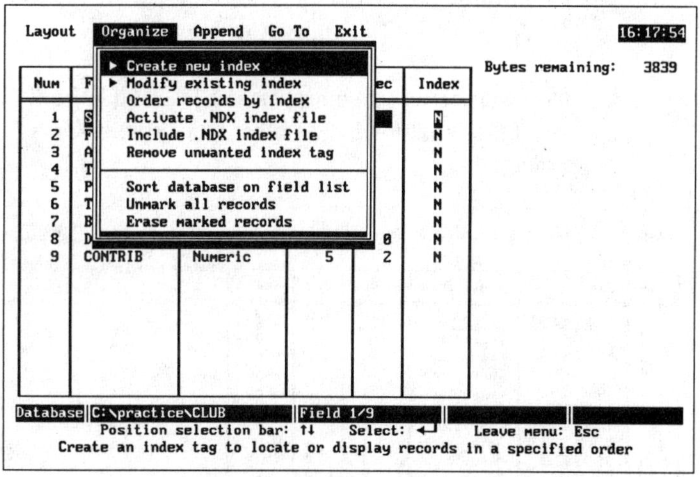

We do not need this menu at the moment.

☞ Press **Esc**.

You can change the entire file structure by means of this screen. You can alter field names and types, add and remove fields etc. We wish to insert a new field called **MEMBERNR** in front of the first field. This is to be a character field (after all, we do not need to make any calculations with these numbers), with a length of 3 characters.

Inserting a field

In the Help line you will see:

```
Insert/Delete field:Ctrl-N/Ctrl-U
```

☞ Ensure that the cursor is positioned in the **SURNAME** field. Then press **Ctrl-N**.

You will see that an empty field is inserted in front of all the other fields. The other fields shift down a place.

A field has been inserted

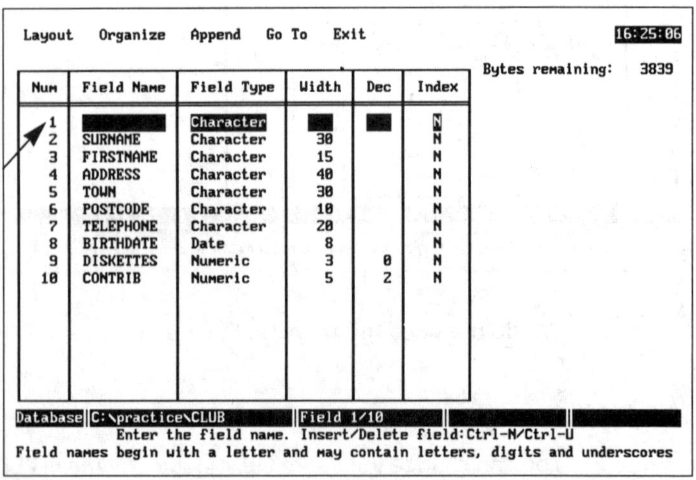

☞ Type **membernr**, press **Enter** twice and type **3**.

Changing the length of the field

We also wanted to shorten a few of the fields.

The field length was shortened so much that the goalposts were offside

☞ Use the ↓ cursor key to move to the **SURNAME** field. Change the length to **18**.
☞ Change the length of the **FIRSTNAME** field to **11**, the **ADDRESS** field to **25** and the **TOWN** to **20**.

This is no trouble at all.

Of course, we want to save these alterations. That can be done using the **Exit** menu. In that case, select the **Save changes and exit** option. But it is quicker to use the key combination **Ctrl-End**.

☞ Press **Ctrl-End**.

A message window appears:

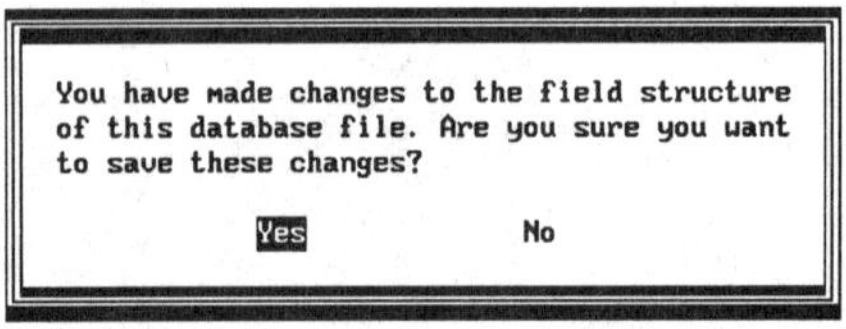

The marking is already positioned on **Yes**.

☞ Press **Enter**.

You will hear some ticking and rattling and you will return to the Control Center. We shall examine the results of our efforts.

☞ Press **F2**.

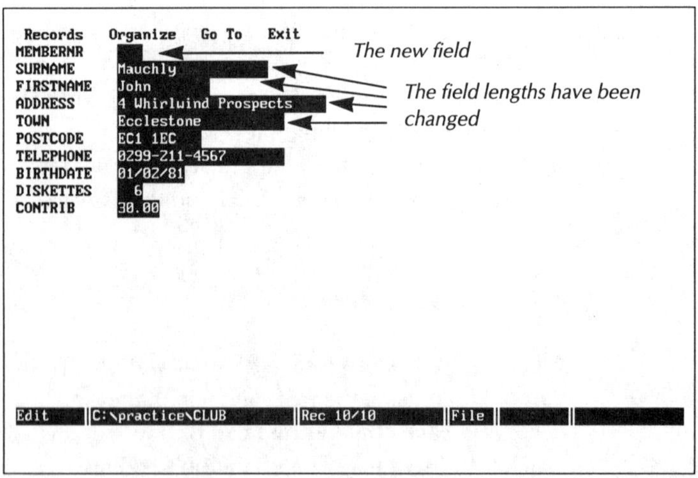

It's all gone smoothly. The record shown is at the end of the file (dBASE has worked through the records). That doesn't matter.

☞ Press **Ctrl-PgUp** to move to the first record. Then press **F2** to activate the browse screen.

The result is just as it should be:

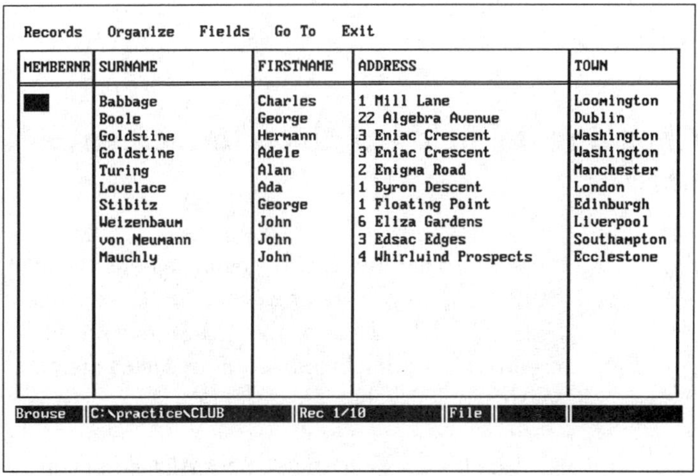

The **MEMBERNR** field has to be filled in of course. The first record should receive number **001**, the second **002** and so on.

☞ Fill in the record numbers.

T

Undoing the changes to a record

If you make changes to a record and you regret it, you can undo the changes. This is easily done as long as you have not moved on to another record. Open the ***Records*** *menu and select* ***Undo change to record****. This is very useful if you have unintentionally changed something in a field and you can't remember exactly what it was.*

Changing the field length on the screen only

There is also another way of gaining a better view of the fields when you are browsing. You can change the lengths of the fields **as they are shown on the screen**. This is done by means of the **Fields** menu. We shall practise this.

☞ Place the cursor in the **SURNAME** field of any record.
☞ Open the **Fields** menu and activate **Size field**.

The Help line indicates that you can change the current column width by means of the ← and → cursor keys.

☞ Press the → cursor key five times. Then press **Enter**.

Note: you have only altered the length of the fields **on the screen**. The file itself remains unchanged.

Moreover, this setting only applies as long as you examine the data. You can easily check this:

☞ Press **Ctrl-End**. You move to the Control Center.
☞ Press **F2**. You will see that the field length shown is the same as the real field length.

T This is where the mouse is handy

The mouse is very useful if you want to increase or decrease the length of fields on the screen. Just place the mouse cursor on the line between two fields. Press and hold down the left mouse button and drag the line to the right or left.

Adding more records

We shall now add a few more records so that we can demonstrate some of the dBASE facilities better. We shall add records from the browse screen.

☞ In the **Browse** screen, move the cursor to record **10** and press the ↓ cursor key.

The following frame appears:

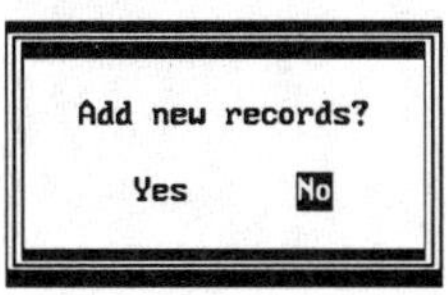

☞ Press the letter **Y**.

The screen then looks like this:

Records   Organize   Fields   Go To   Exit

MEMBERNR	SURNAME	FIRSTNAME	ADDRESS	TOWN
001	Babbage	Charles	1 Mill Lane	Loomington
002	Boole	George	22 Algebra Avenue	Dublin
003	Goldstine	Hermann	3 Eniac Crescent	Washington
004	Goldstine	Adele	3 Eniac Crescent	Washington
005	Turing	Alan	2 Enigma Road	Manchester
006	Lovelace	Ada	1 Byron Descent	London
007	Stibitz	George	1 Floating Point	Edinburgh
008	Weizenbaum	John	6 Eliza Gardens	Liverpool
009	von Neumann	John	3 Edsac Edges	Southampton
010	Mauchly	John	4 Whirlwind Prospects	Ecclestone

Browse | C:\practice\CLUB | Rec EOF/10 | File

Add new records

- ☞ Type **011**. The cursor moves on immediately to the second field (because the MEMBERNR field has been filled).
- ☞ Type **Wilkes** and press **Enter**.
- ☞ Then type the following data, pressing **Enter** where necessary to move the cursor to the next field:

```
Maurice
99 Equation Street
Wilkingston
WK9 4EQ
0544-818-3737
17-12-81
11
10.00
```

When you fill in the contribution (10.00), the cursor jumps back to the MEMBERNR field, in the next (empty) record.

Now enter the following data:

```
012                      013
Freshour                 Hilbert
Ruth                     David
20 Program Place         7 Logic Boulevard
Freshing                 Hilbourne
FR2 1TH                  HB3 8UJ
06614-333-1212           06611-557-13579
03-03-82                 12-11-81
15                       10
7.50                     30.00
```

and:

```
014                      015
Eckert                   Jennings
Presper                  Betty
45 Valve Vales           66 Calculation Grove
Ecclestone               Freshing
EC1 2EC                  FR3 2JN
0299-211-5678            06614-333-2424
13-01-83                 28-05-83
25                       10
12.50                    7.50
```

When you press Enter after you have entered the '7.50' in record 015, the cursor again jumps to the MEMBERNR field to begin a new record. This would be record number 16. However, we only want to use 15 records in the meantime.

☞ Press the ↑ cursor key.

This ensures that all the records, including the last one, are saved.

Searching when there are fields with the same information

We have a few fields which have identical contents. For instance, there are two records in which the TOWN is 'Ecclestone'. When you are searching, how can you be sure that you move to the correct record? Do you have to open the **Go To** menu again and select **Forward search** again? No, there is an easier key combination.

☞ Place the cursor in the **TOWN** field in the first record.
☞ Open the **Go To** menu and select **Forward search**.
☞ Type **Ecclestone** as the search string.
☞ Press **Enter**.

The marking moves directly to Ecclestone in the tenth record.

☞ Now press **Shift-F4**.

You move immediately to Ecclestone in record 14.

In this way, it's very simple.

☞ Now press **Shift-F3**.

In this way, you implement a backwards search for the specified search string.

This method also works when you are examining the data in individual records (thus in the Edit screen).

Searching using wildcards

Imagine you are looking for a name but you have forgotten exactly what the name is. You know that it is something to do with 'love', but was it 'Lovelight' or 'Loverslane' or something else? You can use **wildcards** to help you in the search.

What is a wildcard? It is a character that you can use instead of one or more other characters. You probably know wildcards already from working with MS-DOS. There are two wildcards: the asterisk (*) and the question mark (**?**).

The term 'wildcard' comes from card games. In some card games you can use a wildcard (often a joker) to represent any other card of your choice. For instance, you can lay two aces and a joker instead of three aces. You use the wildcards in the computer in the same way: you use them to represent other characters.

* stands for any number of random characters, such as 'eston' or 'tib' or 'Southa' or '45'. Any characters whatsoever.

? stands for one random character, such as 'j' or 't' or '5' or whatever.

We shall examine just how this works in practice.

- ☞ Press **Ctrl-PgUp** to move to the first record.
- ☞ Make sure the cursor is in the **SURNAME** field.
- ☞ Open the **Go To** menu and select **Forward search**.
- ☞ Enter the search string: **Love*** and press **Enter**.

You see that it works!

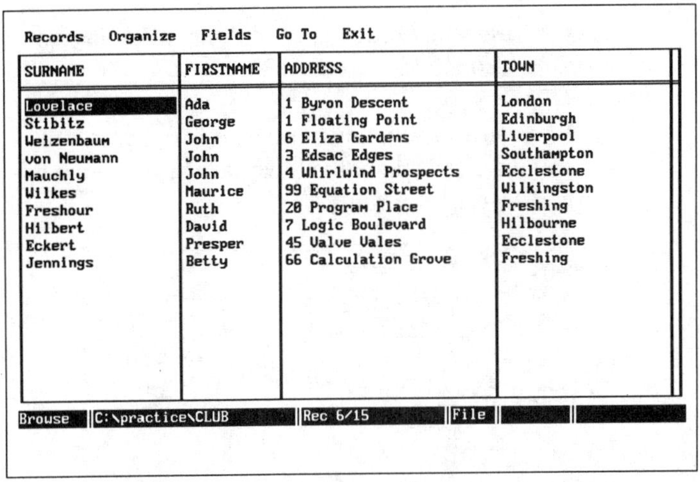

If there had been another record with the name 'Lovegame' or 'Loveisatrickybusiness' before this one, that record would have been found.

As you see, this wildcard is very useful when searching.

The second wildcard is also very useful. It works a little differently. To demonstrate this, we shall first change a place name.

☞ Go to record **3** and change the name of the TOWN to W**i**shing**d**on.
☞ Go to the first record, place the cursor in the **TOWN** field and open the **Go To** menu. Select **Forwards search**.
☞ Type the search string: **W?shing?on**.

The first string which satisfies this condition, 'Wishingdon', is found.

☞ Press **Shift-F4**. The second string, 'Washington' is also found.

You can also combine these types of wildcards. If you were to look for the town **?a?h*g*n** you would find 'Washington'

Wildcards also work when you are busy in the Edit screen.

Deleting a record

We have added a number of records but you can also remove or **delete** records. This always takes place in two stages.

First apply the deletion marking to the record(s) you want to remove. These records are on the nominations list for deletion, as it were, but they are still there. If you have second thoughts, you can simply remove the marking.

If you are sure you really want to delete the records which you have marked, you can proceed. Whether this involves ten records or only one, it will make no difference. Once you have given the deletion command, they are gone forever!

We shall examine how this works. We shall remove the members Wilkes and Hilbert. And for a change we shall do this in the Edit screen.

☞ Press **F2** and press **Ctrl-PgUp** to move to the first record.
☞ Search forwards using the search string **?il***. You are now familiar with this method.

Maurice Wilkes' record appears on the screen.

☞ Open the **Records** menu.

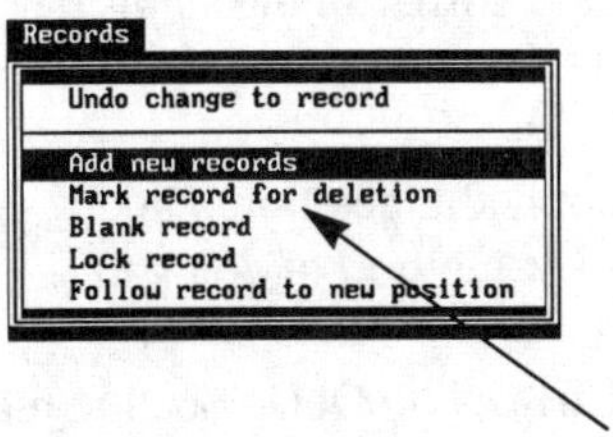

☞ Move the marking bar to **Mark record for deletion**.
☞ Press **Enter**.

The menu disappears again. Maurice Wilkes' record is shown as previously. Has nothing happened?

Have a good look at the status bar. The word **Del** is shown in the right-hand corner. This indicates that this record has been marked for deletion.

☞ Open the **Records** menu again.

You will see that at the position where the **Mark record for deletion** option was situated, the **Clear deletion mark** option is now displayed. The marking bar is also situated there.

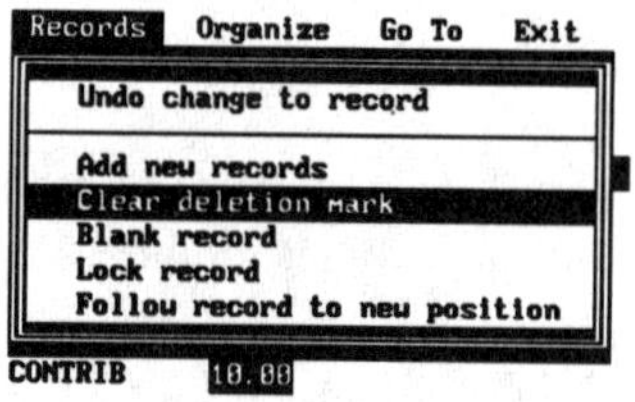

☞ Press **Enter**. As you see the Del indication in the right-hand corner of the status bar has disappeared.

We shall apply the deletion marking again. There is also a quicker method of doing this.

☞ Press **Ctrl-U**. The Del indication reappears.
☞ Press **Ctrl-U** twice again.

In this way, you can switch the deletion marking on and off, just like an electrical switch. The deletion marking should now be on, in other words, Del should be shown on the status bar.

We shall now give David Hilbert's record a deletion mark. We shall demonstrate that this can also be done in the Browse screen.

☞ Press **F2**.
☞ Move the cursor to the **SURNAME** field if necessary. We can find Hilbert by looking for '?il*'.
☞ Press **Shift-F4**.
☞ Then press **Ctrl-U**.

We can now actually delete the records. Keep in mind that you do not need to do this right away. You can wait until next week and carry out all sorts of actions with dBASE in the meantime before you actually delete the records.

With the following actions, it does not matter where the cursor is positioned.

☞ Open the **Organize** menu.

```
Organize  Fields  Go To  Exit
 ▸ Create new index
 ▸ Modify existing index
   Order records by index
   Activate .NDX index file
   Include .NDX index file
   Remove unwanted index tag

   Sort database on field list
   Unmark all records
   Erase marked records
```

☞ Select **Erase marked records**.

As a safeguard question you will be asked if you are sure you want to erase these records:

Are you sure you want to erase all marked records?

Yes No

☞ Select **Yes**.

Goodbye Wilkes and Hilbert. We hope you're happy in any new computer clubs.

Records Organize Fields Go To Exit

SURNAME	FIRSTNAME	ADDRESS	TOWN
Babbage	Charles	1 Mill Lane	Loomington
Boole	George	22 Algebra Avenue	Dublin
Goldstine	Hermann	3 Eniac Crescent	Wishingdon
Goldstine	Adele	3 Eniac Crescent	Washington
Turing	Alan	2 Enigma Road	Manchester
Lovelace	Ada	1 Byron Descent	London
Stibitz	George	1 Floating Point	Edinburgh
Weizenbaum	John	6 Eliza Gardens	Liverpool
von Neumann	John	3 Edsac Edges	Southampton
Mauchly	John	4 Whirlwind Prospects	Ecclestone
Freshour	Ruth	20 Program Place	Freshing
Eckert	Presper	45 Valve Vales	Ecclestone
Jennings	Betty	66 Calculation Grove	Freshing

Browse C:\practice\CLUB Rec 1/13 File

4 Sorting and indexing

We shall add two other records. Because membership numbers 11 and 13 have become available with the departure of Wilkes and Hilbert, we can make use of them again.

☞ Go to the last record and press the ↓ cursor key.
☞ Answer **Yes** to the question **Add new records?**
☞ Enter the following data:

```
003                  011
Frank                Francis
Lawrence             Bilas
3 Memory Lane        12 Code Towers
Lauder               Billingsgate
LD2 5ZD              BG8 22EY
03929-6611           0189-26265
01-06-81             29-04-82
10                   15
10.00                10.00
```

☞ Press the ↑ cursor key if the cursor moves to the MEMBERNR field on the next line.

Changing the order of sequence of the records

We now have a small problem. The membership numbers are no longer in the right order. Fortunately we can do something about this. In fact, it can be rectified in two ways. We can **sort** the file and we can create an **index** for the file.

Why are there two methods available and what is the difference between them?

What is sorting?

You will undoubtedly know this word already. If you sort a dBASE file, that means you make a **copy** of the file. In this copy, the records are placed in a certain order of sequence. You have to tell dBASE how the sorting is to be done. This is done by naming the field according to which the records are to be sorted. For instance, you can specify that the records are to be sorted according to the dates of birth (BIRTHDATE in our case). This means that dBASE will order the records in such a way that the record of the eldest member is placed at the top of the list and the record of the youngest member is placed at the bottom. But you can also sort the records according to SURNAME. In that case, Babbage would still be at the top but new member Bilas would be placed second from the top. You can also reverse the normal alphabetical order (Z to A) so that Weizenbaum is placed at the top and Babbage goes to the bottom.

The order of sequence from small to large (in numeric fields) and A to Z (in character fields) is referred to as **ascending**. In a date field, the ascending order is from an earlier date to a later date.

The reverse order of sequence is referred to as **descending**.

What is an index?

Creating an index, **indexing**, seems very similar to sorting but, in fact, is quite different. With indexing, the **real** order of sequence of the records does not change. It only seems to change. If you have indexed according to surname, the records will be shown in that order when you browse through them. And a useful feature is that if you then add a new record, it will be automatically placed at the correct position (according to surname). But keep in mind: this only **seems** to be the case; the records are actually placed at the end of the file. But when you are using the index, that won't affect you at all.

The attractive thing about indexing is that you can create **several** indexes (for instance, one according to surname, another according to town, one according to date of birth etc.) and that you can switch these indexes on and off as you please.

We shall first practise sorting and then we shall move on to indexing.

A good sort

We shall sort the records according to surname. This means we shall create a **copy** of the file.

☞ Open the **Organize** menu.

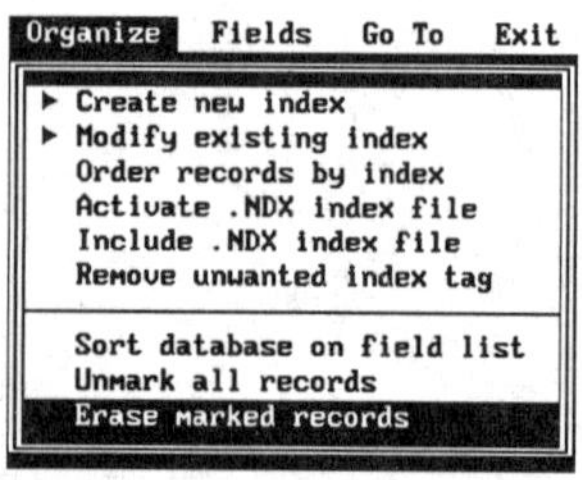

☞ Select **Sort database on field list**.

A frame appears on the screen:

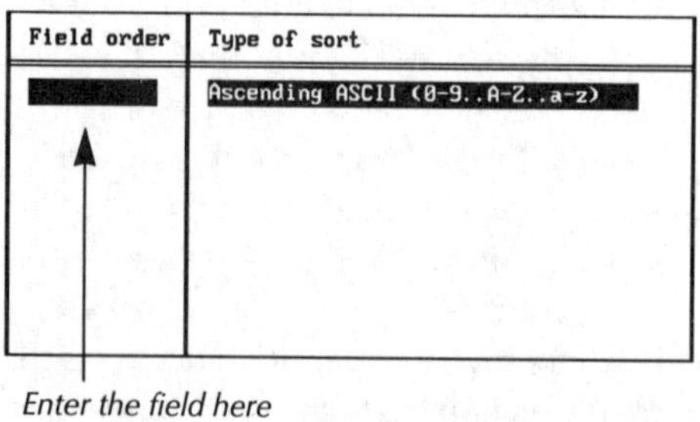

You can specify the sorting field here:

The Help line shows:

```
Pick list:Shift-F1
```

☞ Press **Shift-F1**.

Look how easily the choice can be made. You just select one of the fields presented.

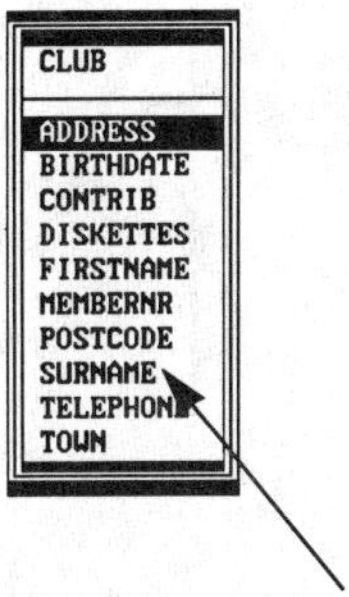

☞ Select **SURNAME**. This field name is adopted into the **Field order** box.

Under **Type of sort** you will see:

```
Ascending ASCII (0-9..A-Z..a-z)
```

This is what we want. But wait a moment. How many 'Goldstines' are there? In which order of sequence should they be placed? Should they be placed in order according to membership number or first name or perhaps date of birth? This is no problem at all. In dBASE, you can sort according to **more than one field**. This means that records are sorted according to the first field you specified, but if there are several records which are the same (as with the Goldstines in our example), dBASE sorts these records according to the second sorting field you specified.

☞ Press the ↓ cursor key. You can specify another field.

☞ Press **Shift-F1** and select **FIRSTNAME**.

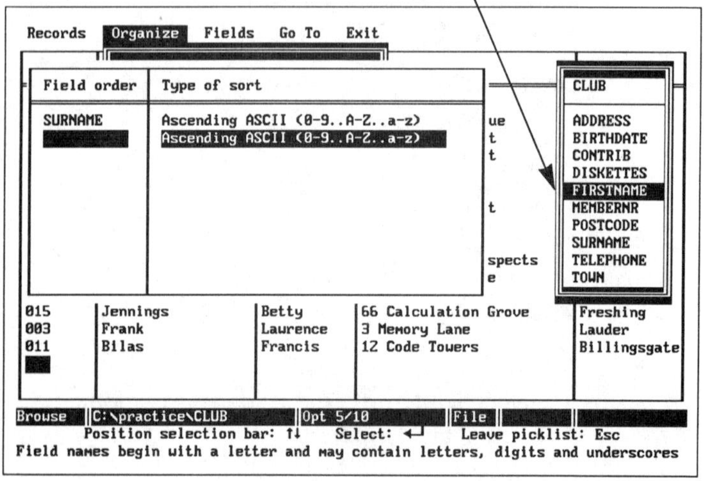

Now the actual sorting can begin. But how?

Look at the Help line. You will see (at the right):

```
Accept:Ctrl-End
```

☞ Press **Ctrl-End**.

Yes, of course, we have to specify a name since you make a **copy** of the database when sorting. And it should receive a different name (you can specify the same name, but if you do, the 'old' database is overwritten with the new one and that is not quite what we want).

☞ Specify **club2** as the name and press **Enter**.

This question ultimately appears:

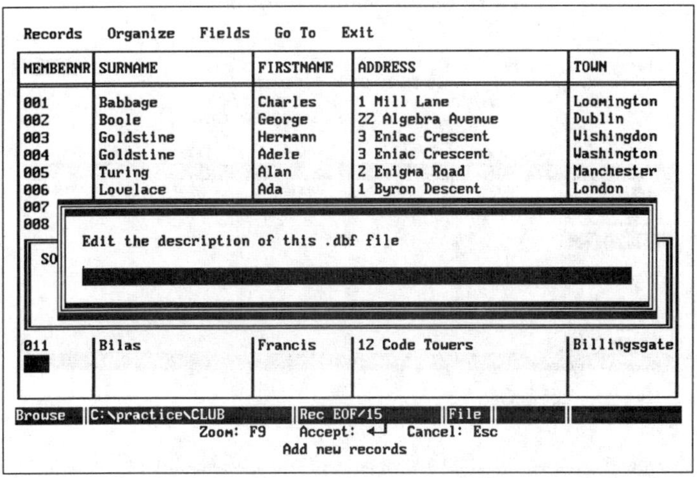

You can link a description to a database. This is shown in the Control Center when you place the marking bar on the name of the database. That can be useful.

☞ Type: **sorted according to surname and first name** and press **Enter**.

And there you are again in the Browse screen. It

seems as if nothing has changed. Has something gone wrong? The reason is that indeed nothing has changed **in this file**. The sorted records have been placed in the new file CLUB2, not in CLUB. Let's have a look in the CLUB2 file.

☞ Press **Esc**.

The **CLUB2** file is now also listed in the **Data** panel.

☞ Move the marking bar to **CLUB2**.

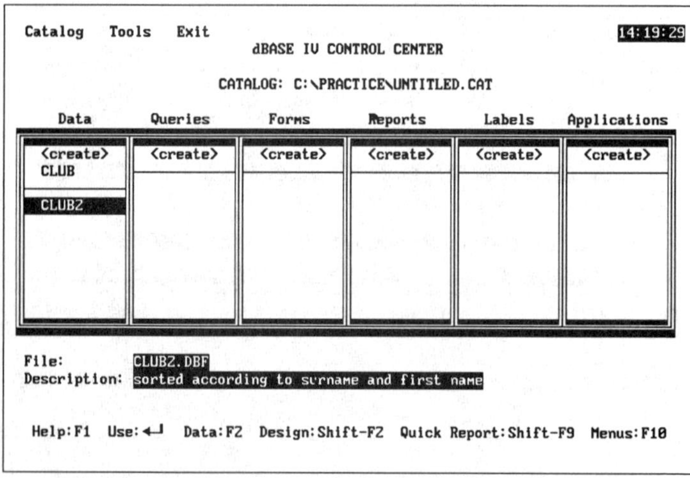

☞ Press **F2**. The file is opened and the browse screen is shown.

You will see that the file has been sorted just as we wanted.

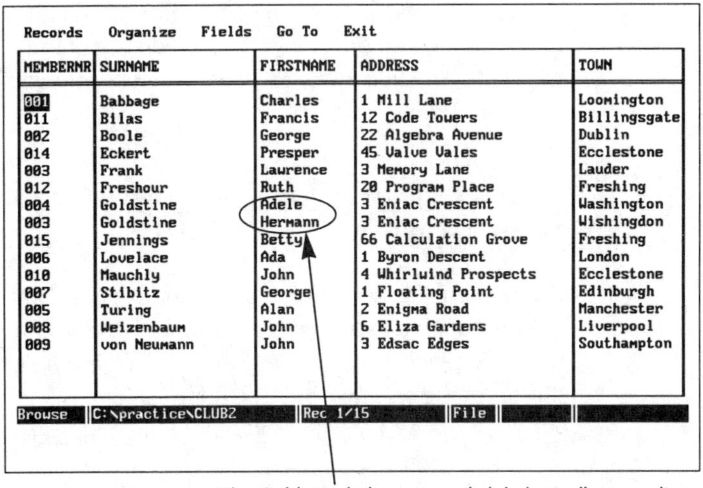

The Goldstine kids are sorted alphabetically according to firstname

The disadvantages of sorting

Despite the fact that this has all taken place smoothly, you might already see that there are some disadvantages to sorting. Imagine you have to add a new member called 'Henry Zoomfunction' to the list. That would be quite convenient in terms of alphabetical order of sequence. But what if the new member is called 'Bert Gates'? You would have to sort the entire list once again. And imagine you wanted to sort the file according to date of birth; you would again have to create a new file. Your Data panel would become rather cluttered.

We shall try indexing

Indexing is almost always more convenient than sorting. When you index a file, you do not change the database itself. An extra companion file is linked to the database, containing information about the order of sequence of the records. You will not even be aware of this extra file.

Moreover, you can switch and index on and off, just like a switch. That is also very useful.

We shall try this out. Let's make an index according to TOWN. If there are several members who live in the same place, they are to be indexed according to surname. We shall use the CLUB file as the basis. We shall leave CLUB2 as it is for the time being.

- ☞ Press **Esc**. You move to the Control Center.
- ☞ Place the marking bar on **CLUB** and press **F2**.
- ☞ Open the **Organize** menu.
- ☞ The marking bar is already positioned on **Create new index**. Press **Enter**.

The following screen appears:

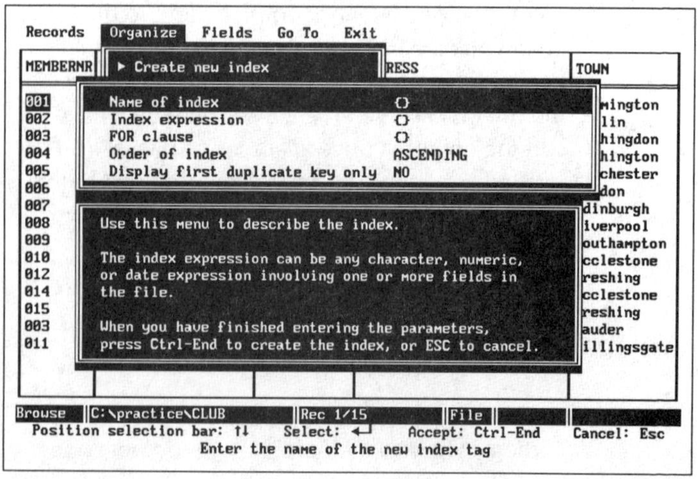

This is also a menu. The two options at the top are the most important in this screen. Firstly, the new index must be given a name:

☞ Make sure that the marking bar is positioned on the **Name of index** option. Press **Enter**.
☞ Type **town** and press **Enter**.

Note: this is **not** the name of the **field**. It is only the name you want to give to the index. You could just as easily have given the name 'xxx', or 'city'. We use the name 'town' because it gives an indication of how the file is indexed.

The marking bar has moved automatically to **Index expression**. What does this mean? This is the **way** the file is to be indexed. This can be a field name, but it can also be something a little more complicated. We shall return to this point later. We want to index the file according to the fields **TOWN** and **SURNAME**. This is done as follows:

☞ Press **Enter**.

The Help line shows:

```
Expression builder: Shift-F1
```

☞ Press the key combination **Shift-F1**.

Another frame is shown on the screen:

Fieldname	Operator	Function
MEMBERNR	#	ABS
SURNAME	$	ACCESS
FIRSTNAME	*	ACOS
ADDRESS	**	ALIAS
TOWN	+	ASC
POSTCODE	-	ASIN
TELEPHONE	->	AT
BIRTHDATE	.AND.	ATAN
DISKETTES	.OR.	ATN2

The field names are shown here, among other things.

☞ Move the marking bar to TOWN and press **Enter**.

This will produce the following result:

Name of index	{TOWN}
Index expression	TOWN
FOR clause	{}
Order of index	ASCENDING
Display first duplicate key only	NO

We haven't finished yet. In cases where there are several members living in the same town, we want to index them according to surname. This is done a little differently than when sorting, but it is just as easy:

☞ Press **Shift-F1** again.
☞ Select + in the list under **Operator**.

The '+' is added to the index expression.

☞ Press **Shift-F1** again and press SURNAME.

The index expression has now become **TOWN+SURNAME**.

```
Name of index                     {TOWN}
Index expression                  TOWN+SURNAME
FOR clause                        {}
Order of index                    ASCENDING
Display first duplicate key only  NO
```

In fact, you could simply have typed this information. But if you use Shift-F1 you are sure that the procedure will always be carried out correctly.

☞ Press **Enter**.

We shall ignore the 'FOR clause'. The other settings in this menu are also as we want to have them. The Help line shows that you can accept the settings by pressing Ctrl-End.

☞ Press **Ctrl-End**.

And what do you see?

Sorted according to town...

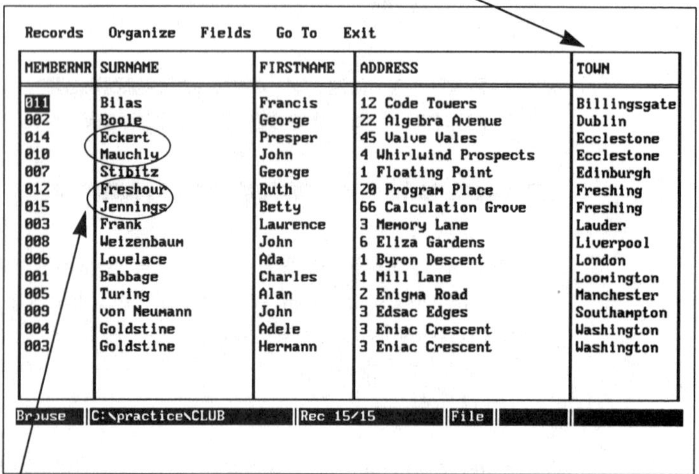

MEMBERNR	SURNAME	FIRSTNAME	ADDRESS	TOWN
011	Bilas	Francis	12 Code Towers	Billingsgate
002	Boole	George	22 Algebra Avenue	Dublin
014	Eckert	Presper	45 Valve Vales	Ecclestone
010	Mauchly	John	4 Whirlwind Prospects	Ecclestone
007	Stibitz	George	1 Floating Point	Edinburgh
012	Freshour	Ruth	20 Program Place	Freshing
015	Jennings	Betty	66 Calculation Grove	Freshing
003	Frank	Laurence	3 Memory Lane	Lauder
008	Weizenbaum	John	6 Eliza Gardens	Liverpool
006	Lovelace	Ada	1 Byron Descent	London
001	Babbage	Charles	1 Mill Lane	Loomington
005	Turing	Alan	2 Enigma Road	Manchester
009	von Neumann	John	3 Edsac Edges	Southampton
004	Goldstine	Adele	3 Eniac Crescent	Washington
003	Goldstine	Hermann	3 Eniac Crescent	Washington

...and then according to surname

☞ Use the ↓ cursor key to move down through the records. Look at the 'Rec' indication on the status bar.

You see that you move from record 15 to record 2 and then on to 12 etc. This indicates that the real order of sequence of records in the file has not been altered. Only the order in which the records are displayed has undergone a change.

Creating more indexes

We shall create two more indexes for this database: one according to membership number and one according to date of birth.

☞ Open the **Organize** menu and select **Create new index**.

☞ Press **Enter** and specify **membernr** as the name and also as the index expression.
☞ Press **Ctrl-End**.

That works no trouble at all as you see.

☞ Now open the **Organize** menu again and select **Create new index.**
☞ Specify **birthdate** as the name and the index expression.

In this index, we want to have the youngest members at the top. This means that we must sort in **descending** order of index.

☞ Move the marking bar to **Order of index** and press the **spacebar**. **ASCENDING** then changes to **DESCENDING**.
☞ Press **Ctrl-End**.

The order of sequence is changed once again. You can check the order by pressing the **Tab** key to move to the BIRTHDATE field.

The youngest member at the top:

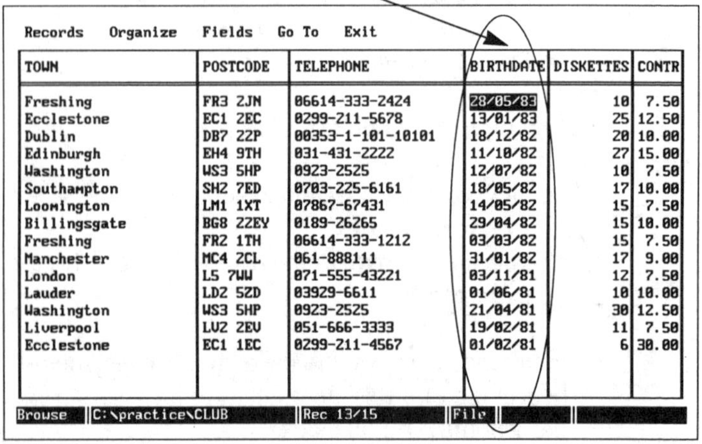

You can switch quickly back and forward from one index to the other.

- ☞ First press **Home** to move to the **MEMBERNR** field (this is not really necessary but it shows clearly what's happening).
- ☞ Open the **Organize** menu and select **Order records by index**.

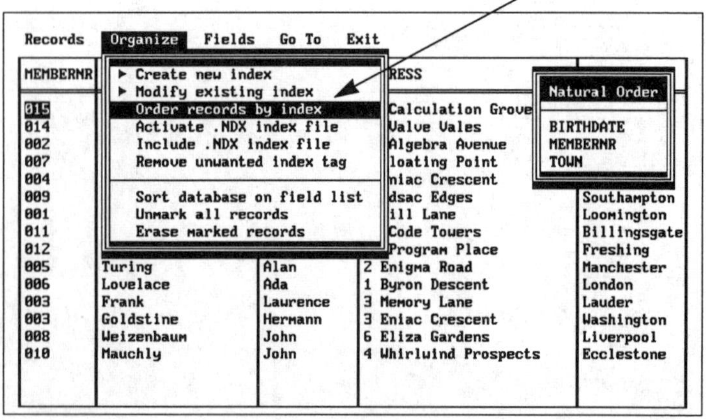

The menu which appears at the right-hand side of the screen contains all the indexes you have made. **Natural Order** is shown above the line. This is the 'real' order of the records, in other words, the order in which the records were created.

☞ Select **Natural Order**.

The records are shown in their original order of sequence.

☞ Now open the **Organize** menu and select **Order records by index**.
☞ Move the marking bar to **TOWN**.

A small frame appears to the left of the menu. The index expression is displayed there:

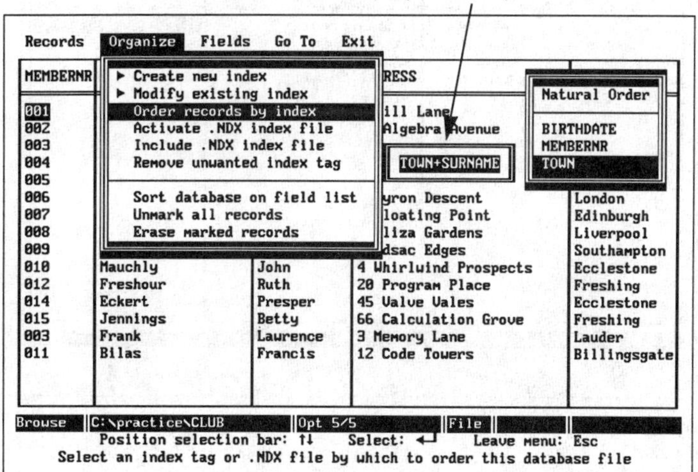

☞ Press **Enter**.

As you see, no trouble at all.

Changing a record while an index is active

If you change a record while a certain index is active, you will see how convenient an index is. Let's examine this.

☞ Go to the **TOWN** field in **Francis Bilas**' record.
☞ Change the name of the town to **R**illingsgate.
☞ Save the change by pressing the → cursor key.

Notice what has happened? The record has been shifted almost to the bottom of the records list. But as you see, it remains record 15 (see the status bar).

Francis is now on top of John

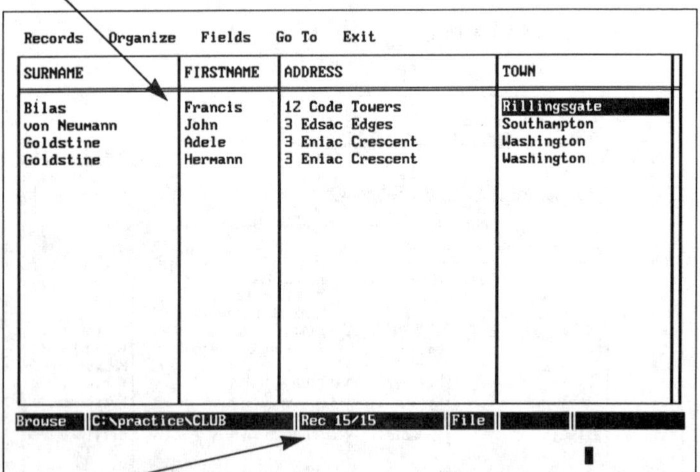

The record number remains the same

As soon as you change anything in the index field, the index is automatically adjusted and the record is moved to the correct position (according to the particular index). Keep in mind that the record is **not really** moved in the basic file.

This is also the case if you add new records. And it also works in this way when you are in the Edit screen.

T You don't want to keep on the move

*If you **do** want to have an index on while you are altering records, but you **don't** want the marking bar to keep jumping about from one position to another, you can switch the marking bar off using the **Records** menu. The last option in this menu is **Follow record to new position**. Normally **Yes** is shown here. If you now move the marking bar to this option and press **Enter**, the **Yes** will change to a **No** (although you won't see this because the menu disappears immediately. From now on, the marking bar will not move when you change the contents of an index field. This works as a switch.*

Searching when an index is active

You can also look for certain information much more quickly by means of an index. You will not really notice this in our practice example, but if you have hundreds of records, the difference in speed can be considerable. Searching has both advantages and disadvantages. One advantage, over and above the speed, is that it does not matter in which field or record the cursor is situated when you begin the search. But the disadvantage is that you can only look for data in the index expression field. If you have specified two or more fields as index expressions, the search will only be performed for the **first** index expression.

Another disadvantage is that wildcards do not work when you are searching in index expressions.

We shall examine how this all works. We shall look for the town **Loomington**.

☞ Press **Ctrl-PgUp** to move to the first record.
☞ Press **Home**.

These actions are not really necessary but we have done this to demonstrate the procedure as clearly as possible.

The currently active index is still **TOWN**. Therefore, when we are using an index expression to carry out the search we can only search for a town. If we wanted to search for a specific date of birth, we would first have to activate the **BIRTHDATE** index.

Open the **Go To** menu and select **Index key search**.

The following window appears on the screen:

☞ Type **Loomington** and press **Enter**.

The cursor finds the appropriate record straight-away.

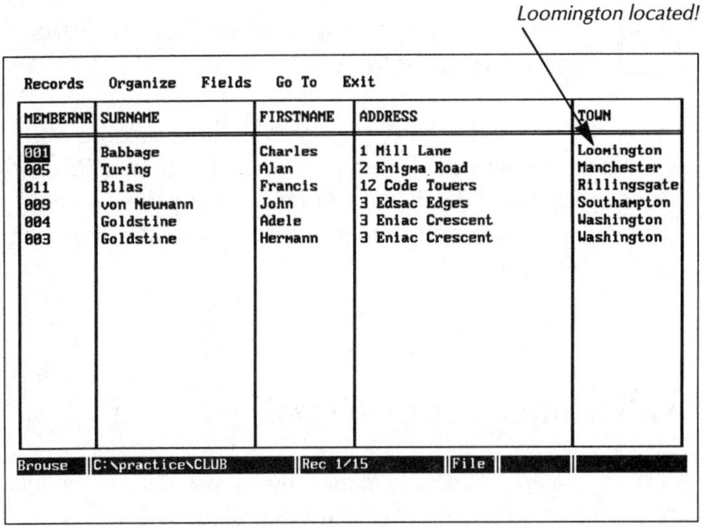

- ☞ Open the **Go To** menu again and select **Index key search**.
- ☞ Type **Dublin** and press **Enter.**

This works wonderfully too. As you see, it makes no difference which field or record you are in when you begin the search. It is not necessary to begin the search **above** the record which is being sought.

Searching according to index expression also works when you are working in the Edit screen.

Creating automatic indexes when defining the structure

*When you create or change the structure of a database file, you can make an index on as many fields as you like. This is done by changing the **N** in the **Index** column in the Design screen, to a **Y**. The index is then automatically given the name of the field.*

Which index is actually active?

If you work with many indexes, you have to pay close attention to **which** index is active. **Unfortunately, you cannot see this on the status bar.** Of course, you can get an idea by examining the order of the records on the screen.

Closing down dBASE again

It's time to close down dBASE again.

- ☞ Press **Esc**. You arrive in the Control Center again.
- ☞ Open the **Exit** menu and select **Quit to DOS**.

We shall now have a look at the contents of the PRACTICE directory.

- ☞ Type **dir** and press **Enter**. If everything has gone properly, you should see the following:

```
*** END RUN    dBASE IV

C:\PRACTICE>dir

 Volume in drive C is GEORGE
 Volume Serial Number is 1B3B-11D8
 Directory of C:\PRACTICE

.            <DIR>         30/09/94    10:28
..           <DIR>         30/09/94    10:28
CATALOG  CAT           439 10/10/94    10:05
UNTITLED CAT           620 10/10/94    12:48
CLUB     DBK         1,942 04/10/94    16:36
CLUB     DBF         2,214 10/10/94    12:41
CLUB2    DBF         2,214 07/10/94    14:14
CLUB     MDX         8,192 10/10/94    12:41
        8 file(s)         15,621 bytes
                     133,435,392 bytes free

C:\PRACTICE>
```

CATALOG.CAT and UNTITLED.CAT are two files which we have seen previously. These are not important right now. The two database files which you made are CLUB.DBF and CLUB2.DBF. The CLUB.**DBK** file is a **backup** file of the CLUB.DBF file. It was made when you changed the structure of CLUB.DBF. Thus, this file contains the old structure. CLUB.MDX is the index file. It contains the various indexes which you created. If you save the CLUB database file on diskette, you should really copy the CLUB.MDX index file too.

5 Putting the data on paper

Of course, you will at one time or another want to place your information on paper. It is, for instance, useful to have a list of club members, sorted alphabetically according to surname.

When you want to print data, you first have to open the required file.

☞ Start up dBASE and open the **CLUB** file. This is done by placing the marking bar in the **Data** panel on the file and pressing **Enter**. Then select **Use file**.
☞ Press the → cursor key three times.

A report

The marking bar should now be positioned on **<create>** in the **Reports** panel. This is the panel which deals with printing. (Don't think about your school report here, there's enough time for misery in the future! This report has nothing to do with that.)

☞ Press **Enter**. The following screen appears:

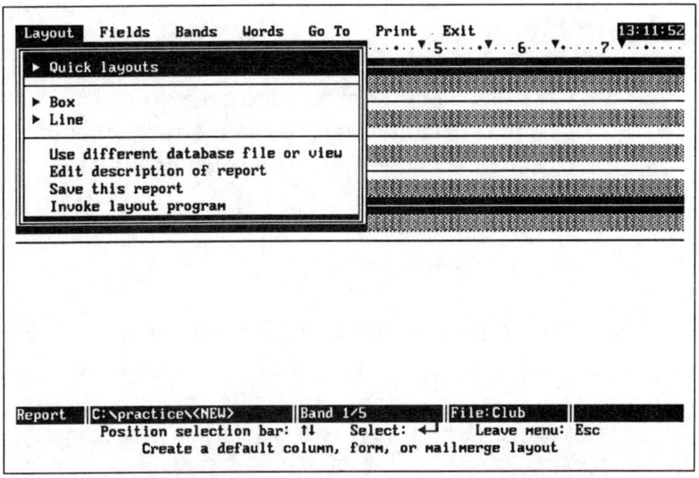

The **Layout** menu is automatically opened. The marking bar is situated on the **Quick layouts** option. This is what we need.

☞ Press **Enter**.

A second menu opens:

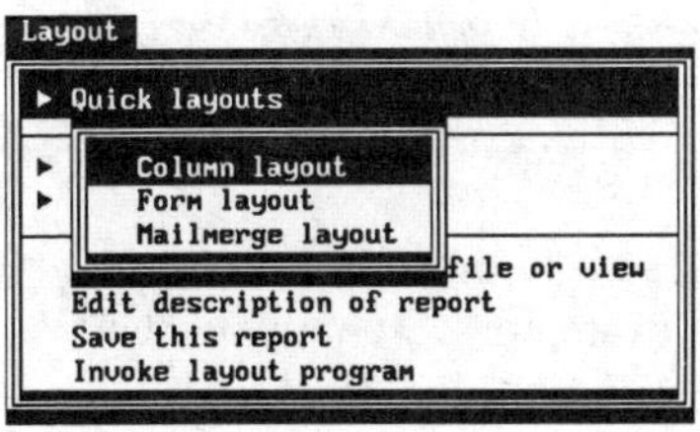

Column layout

Here too, the first option is the one we need: Column layout. This means that the data will be placed next to one another in columns, just as in the Browse screen.

☞ Press **Enter**.

This produces a rather remarkable screen!

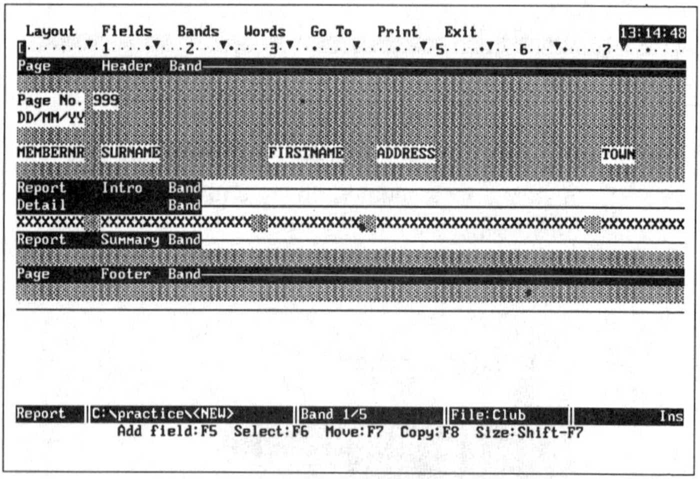

What does this represent?
Let's first examine what happens when we open the **Print** menu from the menu bar.

The first printout

☞ Open the **Print** menu.
☞ Select **Destination**.

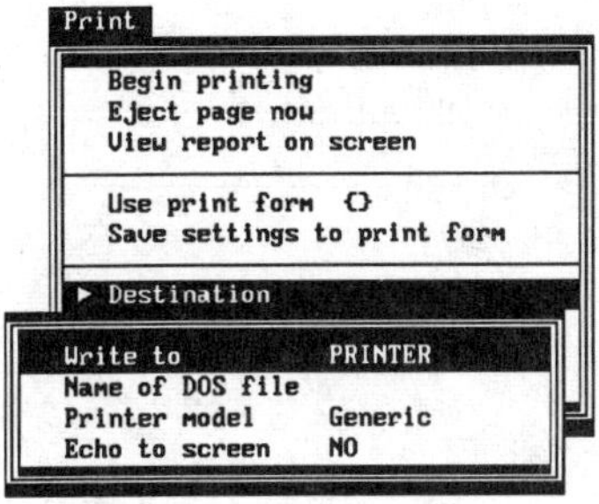

In the small menu which has just been opened, the word **PRINTER** should be shown behind the words **Write to**. If that is not so, press the spacebar.

- ☞ Now press **Esc**.
- ☞ Make sure the printer is switched on, that it is 'online' and that there is sufficient paper.
- ☞ Select **Begin printing**.

Printing to a file

*If you do not have a printer or if you prefer to do the layout in WordPerfect for instance, you can then **write to a file**. In that case, once you have activated the **Destination** option from the **Print** menu, ensure that the word **FILE** is shown behind the words **Write to** (press the spacebar if necessary). Then move the marking bar to **Name of DOS file**, press **Enter** and type the name you want to give the new file. Move the marking bar to the next option, **Printer model**, and make sure that **ASCII Text** is shown here (press the spacebar if necessary). Press **Esc** to return to the **Print** menu and then select **Begin printing**. The data are not sent to the printer, they are sent to the file you specified. You can then load this file in WordPerfect when required.*

Your version may look a little different, but the result is not terribly attractive.

```
Page No.    1 10/10/94
MEMBERNR  SURNAME            FIRSTNAME     ADDRESS                  TOWN
POSTCODE    TELEPHONE            BIRTHDATE  DISKETTES  CONTRIB


001         Babbage            Charles       1 Mill Lane              Loomington
LM1 1XT     07867-67431          14/05/82    15          7.50
002         Boole              George        22 Algebra Avenue        Dublin
DB7 22P     00353-1-101-10101    18/12/82    20         10.00
003         Goldstine          Hermann       3 Eniac Crescent         Washington
WS3 5HP     0923-2525            21/04/81    30         12.50
004         Goldstine          Adele         3 Eniac Crescent         Washington
WS3 5HP     0923-2525            12/07/82    10          7.50
005         Turing             Alan          2 Enigma Road            Manchester
MC4 2CL     061-88811            31/01/82    17          9.00
006         Lovelace           Ada           1 Byron Descent          London
L5 7WW      071-555-43221        03/11/81    12          7.50
007         Stibitz            George        1 Floating Point         Edinburgh
EH4 9TH     031-431-2222         11/10/82    27         15.00
008         Weizenbaum         John          6 Eliza Gardens          Liverpool
LV2 2EV     051-666-3333         19/02/81    11          7.50
009         von Neumann        John          3 Edsac Edges            Southampton
SH2 7ED     0703-225-6161        18/05/82    17         10.00
010         Mauchly            John          4 Whirlwind Prospects    Ecclestone
EC1 1EC     0299-211-4567        01/02/81     6         30.00
012         Freshour           Ruth          20 Program Place         Freshing
FR2 1TH     06614-333- 1212      03/03/82    15          7.50
014         Eckert             Presper       45 Valve Vales           Ecclestone
EC1 2EC     0299-211-5678        13/01/83    25         12.50
015         Jennings           Betty         66 Calculation Grove     Freshing
FR3 2JN     06614-333-2424       28/05/83    10          7.50
003         Frank              Lawrence      3 Memory Lane            Lauder
LD2 5ZD     03929-6611           01/06/81    10         10.00
011         Bilas              Francis       12 Code Towers           Rillingsgate
BG8 22EY    0189-26265           29/04/82    15         10.00
240    164.00
```

Why has the file become so ragged? dBASE has simply placed all the fields next to one another and the records under one another (this is the 'column layout'). But because the lines are longer than the paper is wide, the lines are wrapped to the following line. In fact, you would have to have very wide paper (or very small letters) to get everything neatly on paper. The following page shows how that would look (not in the length but in the breadth).

Let's see if we can do something about this. Firstly we have to have a closer look at the Report screen.

Page No. 1

10/10/94

MEMBERNR	SURNAME	FIRSTNAME	ADDRESS	TOWN	POSTCODE	TELEPHONE	BIRTHDATE	DISKETTES	CONTRIB
001	Babbage	Charles	1 Mill Lane	Loomington	LM1 1XT	07867-67431	14/05/82	15	7.50
002	Boole	George	22 Algebra Avenue	Dublin	DB7 22P	00353-1-101-10101	18/12/82	20	10.00
003	Goldstine	Hermann	3 Eniac Crescent	Washington	WS3 5HP	0923-2525	21/04/81	30	12.50
004	Goldstine	Adele	3 Eniac Crescent	Washington	WS3 5HP	0923-2525	12/07/82	10	7.50
005	Turing	Alan	2 Enigma Road	Manchester	MC4 2CL	061-888111	31/01/82	17	9.00
006	Lovelace	Ada	1 Byron Descent	London	L5 7WW	071-555-43221	03/11/81	12	7.50
007	Stibitz	George	1 Floating Point	Edinburgh	EH4 9TH	031-431-2222	11/10/82	27	15.00
008	Weizenbaum	John	6 Eliza Gardens	Liverpool	LV2 2EV	051-666-3333	19/02/81	11	7.50
009	von Neumann	John	3 Edsac Edges	Southampton	SH2 7ED	0703-225-6161	18/05/82	17	10.00
010	Mauchly	John	4 Whirlwind Prospects	Ecclestone	EC1 1EC	0299-211-4567	01/02/81	6	30.00
012	Freshour	Ruth	20 Program Place	Freshing	FR2 1TH	06614-333-1212	03/03/82	15	7.50
014	Eckert	Presper	45 Valve Vales	Ecclestone	EC1 2EC	0299-211-5678	13/01/83	25	12.50
015	Jennings	Betty	66 Calculation Grove	Freshing	FR3 2JN	06614-333-2424	28/05/83	10	7.50
003	Frank	Lawrence	3 Memory Lane	Lauder	LD2 5ZD	03929-6611	01/06/81	10	10.00
011	Bilas	Francis	12 Code Towers	Rillingsgate	BG8 22EY	0189-26265	29/04/82	15	10.00

The Report screen

You will see that the screen is divided by horizontal lines into a number of sections. These sections are called **bands**. The beginning of a section contains the words **Header Band** or **Intro Band** for instance.

Only a few of these bands are of interest to us at this moment. The most important band is the **Detail Band**. The contents of this band represent the contents of the fields in the various records. We shall examine this more closely.

The Detail Band

- ☞ Move the cursor (the flashing block at the P in 'Page Header Band') downwards until it is situated in one of the Xs under the word 'Detail'.
- ☞ Look at the bottom Help line:

```
CLUB->MEMBERNR    Type: Character    Width:   3     Decimal:  0
```

This means that instead of the Xs, the contents of the MEMBERNR field in the CLUB file will be printed on paper. And because this is the 'column layout', all the membership numbers will be printed **under one another** at that position. You have seen this in our illustration. Thus, the Xs represent **all** the contents of the MEMBERNR field.

The same applies to the other Xs more to the right on the screen. Move the cursor in that direction. The Help line shows that the next series of Xs represents the SURNAME field. In this way, all the fields in the CLUB file are represented by Xs.

Templates

The fact that these are not just common Xs can be shown by moving the cursor in the group of Xs. You cannot just move to one particular X; you are situated on all the Xs at once. We refer to this field indication as a **template**.

In this column layout, dBASE has automatically placed a template for each field. What else has dBASE placed in this structure?

The Page Header Band

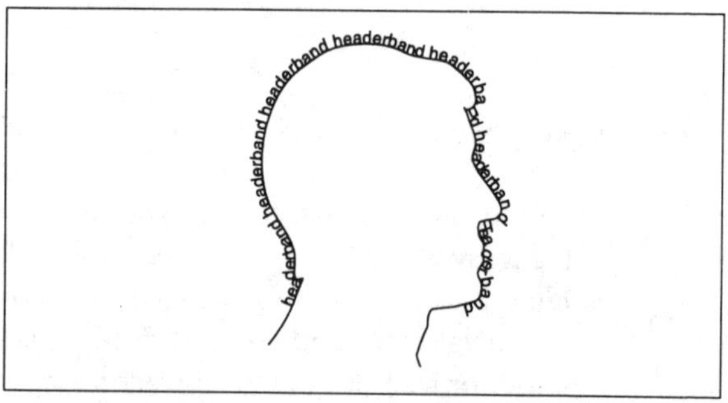

Trouble with headerband? Buy an electric razor

At the top of the screen, under the menus, you will see the **Page Header Band**. The text shown here will be printed at the top of each page. The '999' which is shown here is a kind of template or code.

This template prints the page number on each page; the number is increased by one each time. The present dBASE settings will produce the following text on each page:

```
Page No.  1  (this number is automatically increased)
14-10-94  (this is the date of printing)

(all the field names will be placed here)
```

Of course, the page number will only be increased if the file contains so many records that they do not all fit onto one page.

The registration 'DD/MM/YY' is also a template. The date will be printed at this position.

You can easily check that the date and the page numbering are templates:

- ☞ Press the cursor keys to move to **DD/MM/YY**. You will see that all these characters become marked. If you glance at the Help line you will see **DATE**.
- ☞ Go to the words **Page No.** You will see that the cursor only marks the letter on which it is positioned. The Help line at the bottom is empty.
- ☞ Go to the **999** template. You will recognise that this is a template.
- ☞ Now move a little further to the right and type **Good Morning!**

This message is also displayed in the Page Header Band.

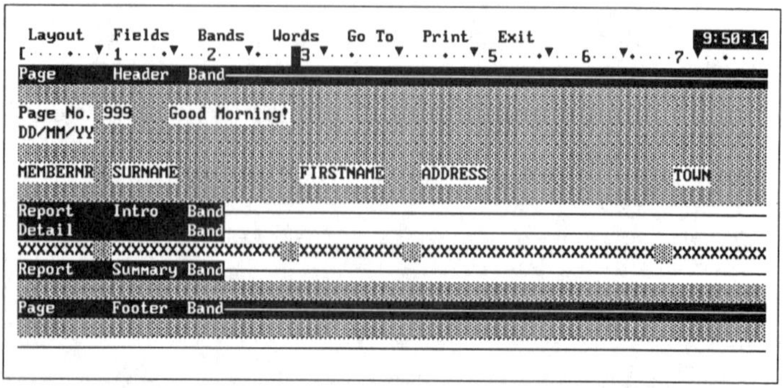

Removing templates and text

Templates and text can also be easily removed:

- ☞ Place the cursor on **999** and press **Del**.
- ☞ Press **Backspace** a number of times until **Page No.** is completely deleted.
- ☞ Move the cursor to **DD/MM/YY** and press **Del**.

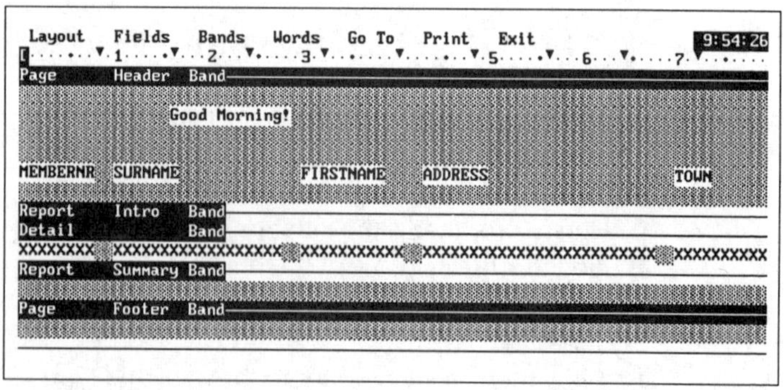

The Report Summary Band

The Report Summary Band is a very interesting section. Here, you can add the contents of the numeric fields in the database together.

☞ Go to the Report Summary Band (the line under the text) and press **End**.
☞ Press the ← cursor key.

You will see that a **9999.99** template is marked. This is not the contribution template; that is shown in the Detail Band, one line above this one.

☞ Look at the Help line. It shows:

```
Operation: SUM   Summarize: CONTRIB
```

This means that all values in the CONTRIB field are added up here. Take a look at the figure on page 132. There the contribution, totalling **164.00**, is shown instead of the template. Thus, a total of **164** pounds has been paid in contribution. That is very useful to know!

The template next to this one indicates the total number of diskettes that the members possess: 240.

Making your own layout

We have now discovered a couple of facts:

1. In this layout, there are too many fields to be able to create an attractive layout.

2. We can use various templates.

We could adjust this layout to our own wishes, but we can also create our own layout. To do that, we first have to quit this layout.

☞ Press **Esc**.
☞ Answer **Y** to the question **Are you sure you want to abandon operation?**.

You return to the Control Center. The marking bar is still positioned on **<create>** in the **Reports** panel.

☞ Press **Enter**.
☞ This time do not select **Quick layout** like you did the last time; press **Esc**.

This produces an empty design screen so that we can begin creating our own layout.

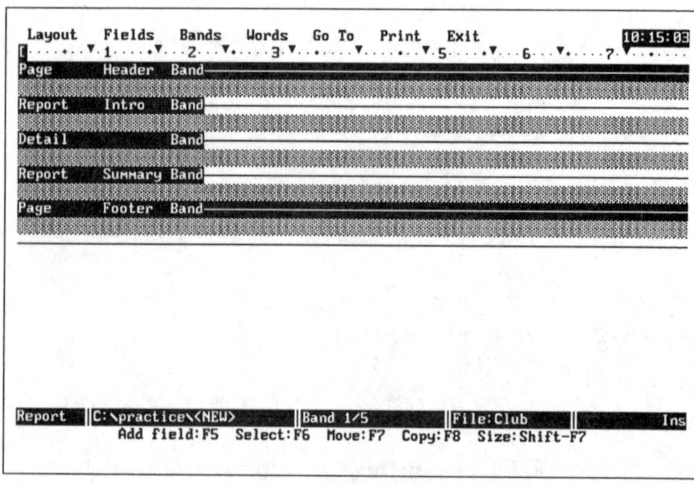

What do we actually want to print?

We should first consider what exactly we want to print. We want a list of all members, sorted alphabetically according to surname. We also want the first letter of the first name, followed by a dot, to be placed in front of the surname. This should be followed by the town, telephone number and the contribution. That will be enough for now.

Defining the header

We want to have the text **"The Mammoth" computer club - list of members** placed in the header at the top of the page. This text should be in boldface.

☞ Press the Cursor Down key to move the cursor to the Page Header Band (the area under these words).

☞ Open the **Words** menu and select **Style**.

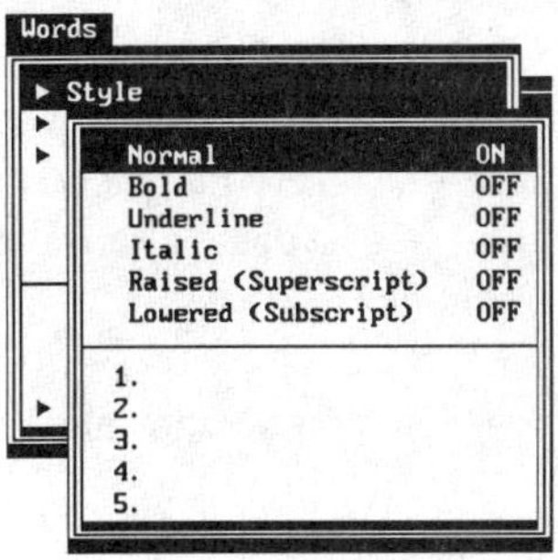

☞ Move the marking bar to **Bold** and press **Enter**.

☞ Type **"The Mammoth" computer club - list of members**.

That was the header. Now we have to place the templates for the fields. That is done in the Detail Band.

☞ Move the cursor to the left edge of the Detail Band.

T ***Pay attention when applying bold, underlining, italics etc.***

The options in the ***Style*** *menu only work properly if dBASE 'knows' what kind of computer you are working with. This will have been specified when dBASE was installed on your computer (or should have been). If printing does not take place as it should, ask someone to have a look at the printer settings.*

Placing the templates

We cannot just begin by typing FIRSTNAME. dBASE will only see this as text. We want it to represent the database field which is to be placed in this report. Therefore, we have to place a **template** here. That is done quite simply:

☞ Open the **Fields** menu and select **Add field**.

The choice is yours:

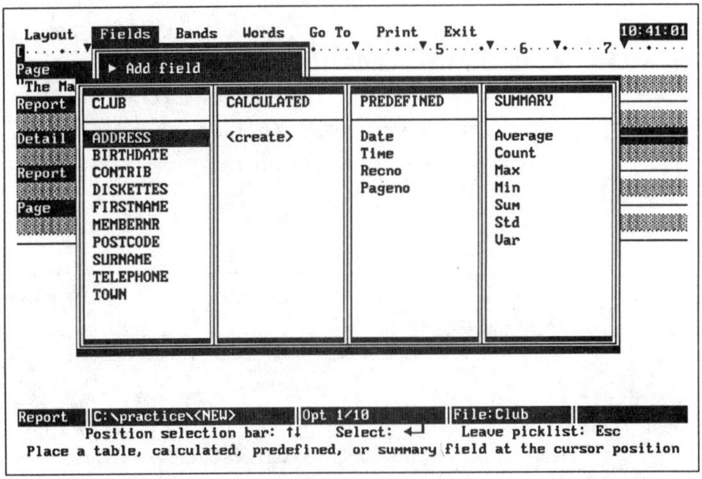

In addition to the field names, other templates such as Pageno and Date and Sum with which we are already familiar are also shown in the other panels.

The marking is on Template

☞ Move the marking bar to **FIRSTNAME** and press **Enter**.

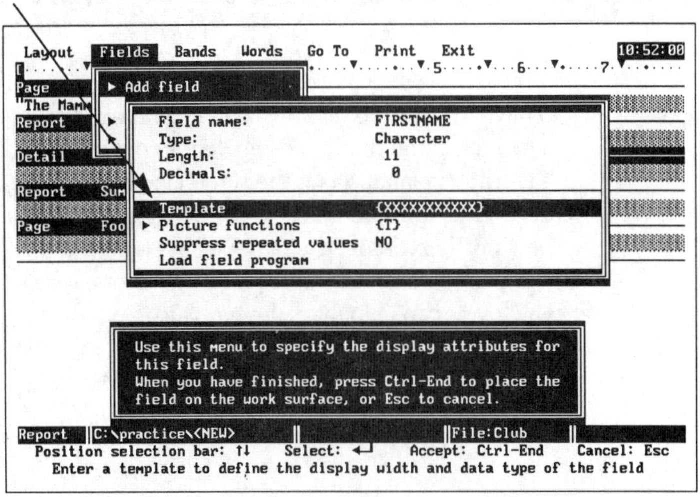

Oh oh, this looks rather complicated. But in fact, it's not really so difficult. The marking bar is on **Template**. These are the familiar Xs. When you were working with **numeric** fields, you saw that **nines** were used in the template.

☞ Press **Enter**.

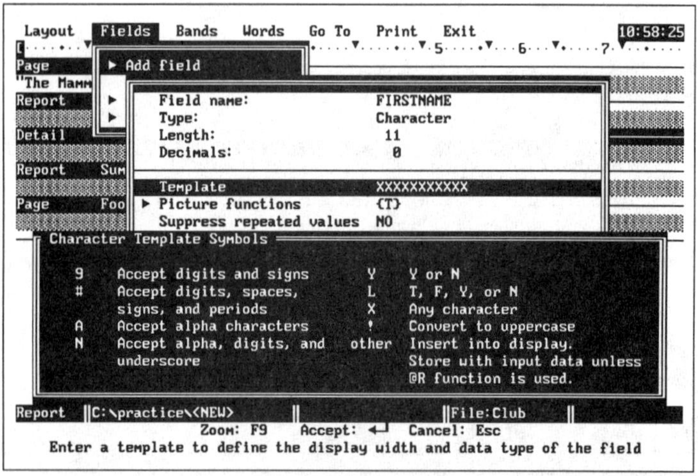

You can now specify the kind of template you want to have. dBASE has already filled in a number of Xs; in fact the same number as the length of the field (11). The explanation on the screen indicates that X represents 'any character'. If you were to replace the Xs with exclamation marks, all the letters in this field would be printed in capitals. This is one way in which you can influence the template.

But in our example, we only want one X. We only want to print the first letter of the first name.

☞ Press the **Backspace** key 10 times. Only one X remains.

☞ Press **Enter**. Template now shows **{X}**.

As the information indicates, pressing Ctrl-End will place the field on the work surface (as dBASE calls it).

☞ Press **Ctrl-End**.

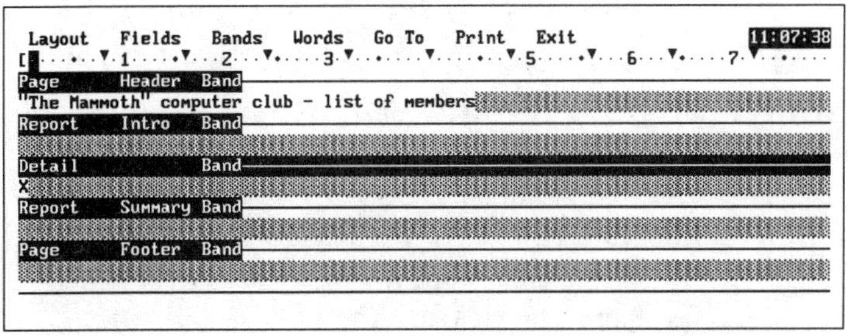

All that trouble for one X! Well, you have to put some effort into learning. And, as you see, it isn't that difficult.

☞ Type a dot to the right of the X. The cursor moves on to the third position on the line.

☞ Move the cursor one position to the right.

Now the SURNAME field should be placed here. It's not really necessary to select **Add field** from the **Fields** menu. There is a shortcut key combination available to perform this action much more quickly. This is shown in the Help line.

☞ Press **F5** and select **SURNAME**.

☞ This template is alright; we do not need to abbreviate it. Simply press **Ctrl-End**.

☞ Move the cursor one position to the right.
☞ Press **F5** again and select **TOWN**.
☞ Press **Ctrl-End**.

And now the telephone number.

☞ Move the cursor one position to the right.
☞ Press **F5** again and select **TELEPHONE**.
☞ Press **Ctrl-End**.

Shortening a template

Well, this is looking fine. We could perhaps shorten the town template just a little. After all, the names of the towns are not really lengthy. This will be no problem. The Help line shows:

```
Size:Shift-F7
```

☞ Move the cursor to the **TOWN** template (the Help line always provides information about the templates).
☞ Press **Shift-F7**.
☞ Press the ← cursor key five times and then **Enter**.

A piece of cake! But there is now quite a lot of space between the TOWN and the TELEPHONE number. But that can be easily resolved.

Moving a template

The Help line shows:

```
Select:F6 Move:F7
```

You might think that you have to press **F7**, but that is not so. If you want to move a template, you first have to **select** it using **F6**.

☞ Move the cursor to the **TELEPHONE** template and press **F6**.

In fact, you can select much more by simply moving the cursor in a certain direction. But that is not what we want at the moment.

☞ Press **Enter** to confirm the selection (also shown in the Help line) and then press **F7**.

☞ Press the ← cursor key five times. A kind of 'shadow' moves leftwards.

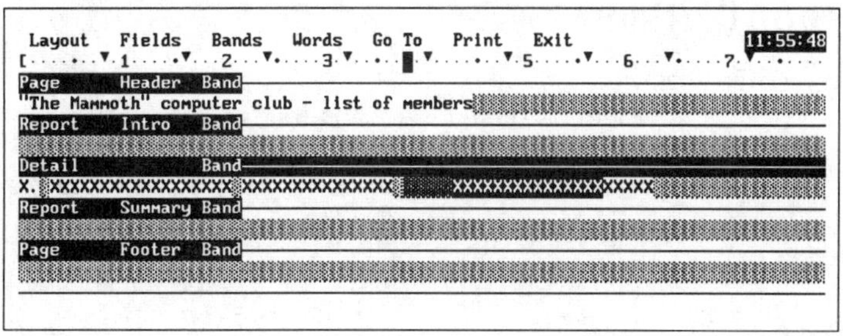

☞ Press **Enter** and answer **Y** to the question **Delete covered text and fields?**.

We shall enter the contribution as the last template.

- ☞ Move the cursor to the appropriate position (leave **2** blank spaces between these fields) and press **F5**.
- ☞ Select **CONTRIB** and press **Ctrl-End**.

> ***Movable fields***
>
> *When you entered these fields in the Detail Band, you 'fixed' them at a certain place by pressing the → cursor key to move on to the next field. If you use the spacebar instead of the → cursor key to move on to the next field, any later adjustment to the size of a field will result in the other field(s) automatically shifting over in accordance with the changes.*

Templates for the average and the total contribution

It would be quite interesting to display the average and the total club contribution.

- ☞ Place the cursor in the Report Summary Band and press **Enter**. There are now two lines in this section.
- ☞ Place the cursor in the second of these lines, exactly under the CONTRIBUTION template.
- ☞ Press **F5** and select **Average** from the SUMMARY panel.

- ☞ A menu appears. Move the marking bar to **Field to summarize on** and press **Enter.** The marking bar is already on **CONTRIB**. Select it.
- ☞ Now move the marking bar to **Template**, press **Enter** and the **Home**.
- ☞ The cursor is at the beginning of this field. Press **Del** to remove the first five nines. Then press **Enter**.

The frame should now look like this:

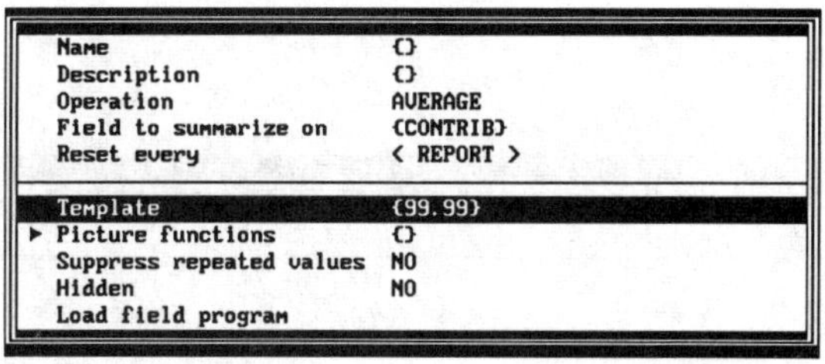

- ☞ Press **Ctrl-End**.
- ☞ Press the ← cursor key nine times and type the word **Average:**.
- ☞ Then move the cursor to the right of the template and press **Enter**. Another new line is added to this section.
- ☞ Type the word **Total:** under **Average:**. Press the → cursor key twice to leave two positions blank and create a field for the total contribution. This is done by pressing F5 and selecting **Sum**. Then move to **Field to summarize on**, press **Enter** and select **CONTRIB**. Move to **Template**. Press **Enter, Home** and **Del** to leave *three* numbers in front of the decimal point.
- ☞ Press **Enter** and then **Ctrl-End**.

The result should be like this:

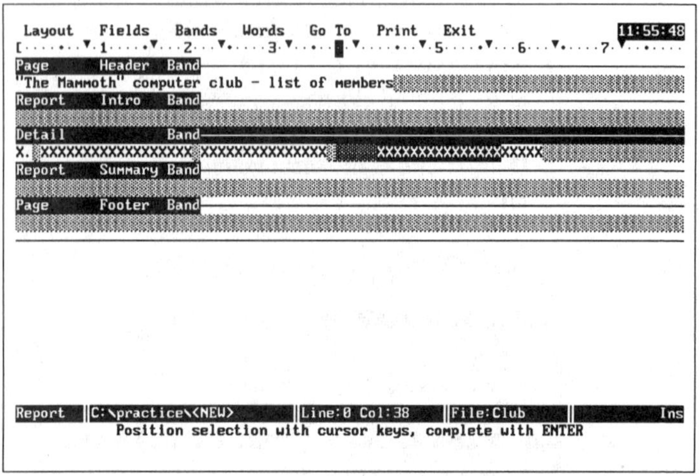

At last!

Our layout is complete. We can begin printing. But wait a moment: didn't we want to have the list sorted alphabetically according to surname? We shall have to index the file first because this index does not yet exist. Back to the database.

We can save this 'report design', as it is called, for use later.

☞ Open the **Exit** menu and select **Save changes and exit**.

☞ You have to give a name to this design.

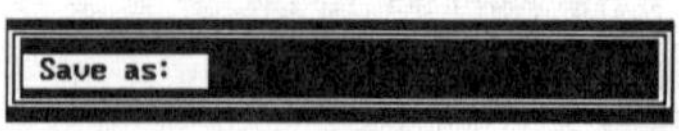

☞ Type **names** and press **Enter**.

And one more question.

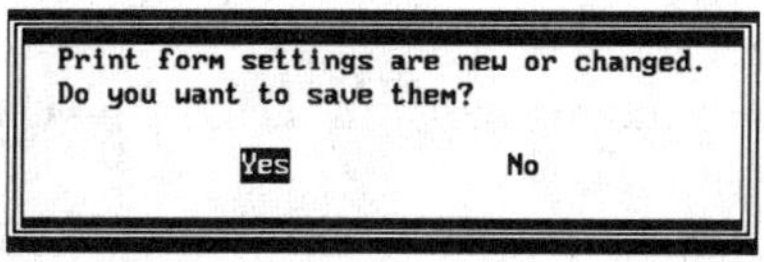

☞ Type **y**.

Is there no end?

☞ Press **Enter**.

And there is the name of our report design, neatly displayed in the **Reports** panel.

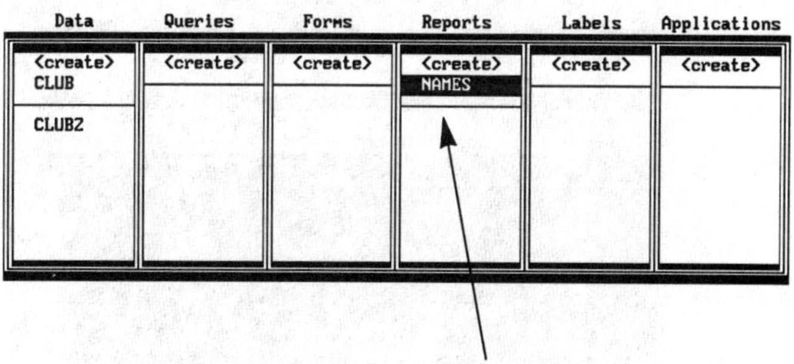

Neatly displayed

Indexing on surnames

Making the index on the surnames is of course a piece of cake:

- ☞ Place the marking on **CLUB** in the **Data** panel.
- ☞ Press **F2**.
- ☞ Open the **Organize** menu and select **Create new index**.
- ☞ The marking is on **Name of index**. Press **Enter** and type **surnames**.
- ☞ Move the marking to **Index expression**, press **Enter** and press **Shift-F1**.
- ☞ Place the marking on **SURNAME** and press **Enter**.

We shall specify the TOWN as the second part of the index key.

- ☞ Type a **+** and press **Shift-F1**.
- ☞ Select **TOWN** and press **Enter**.

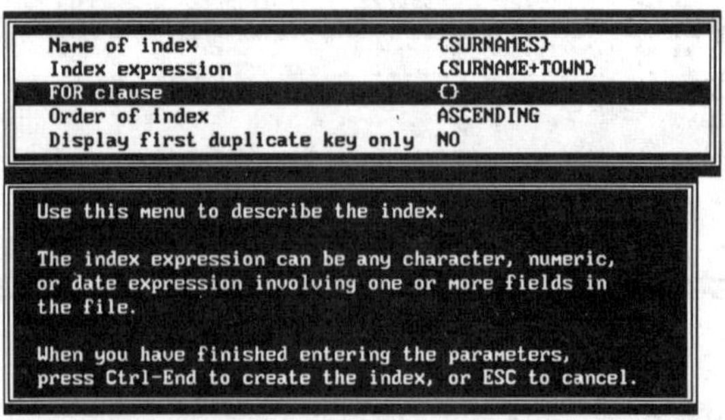

- ☞ Press **Ctrl-End**.

The index comes into force immediately as you see.

Back to the report design

We can finally begin printing. But first back to the report design.

☞ Press **Esc**, place the marking on **NAMES** in the **Reports** panel and press **Enter**.

You can now choose one of three options:

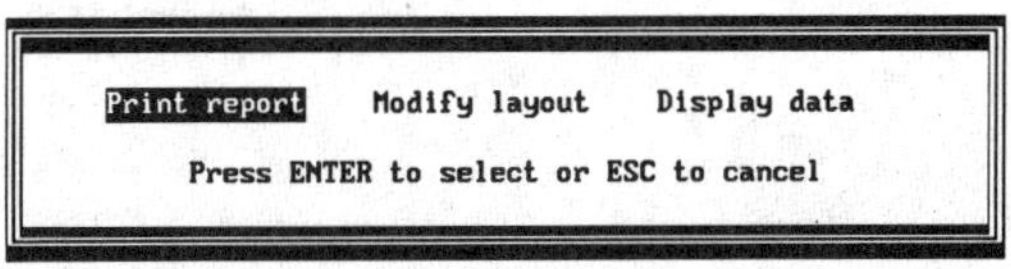

If you choose **Modify layout**, you will move to the design screen. We assume that is no longer necessary.

☞ Select **Print report**.

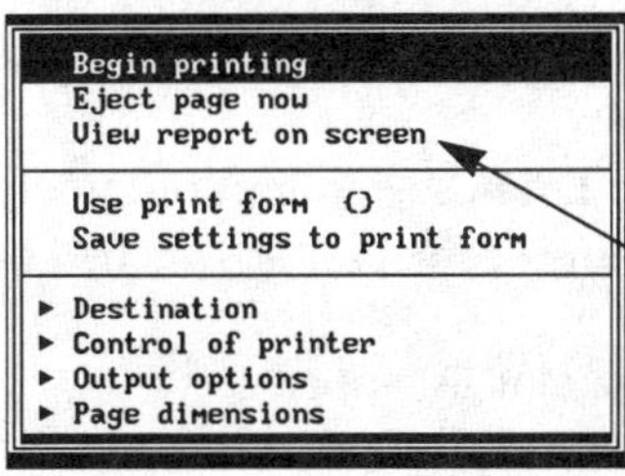

You are already familiar with the menu that now appears. We shall try the **View report on screen** option first.

☞ Select **View report on screen**.

```
"The Mammoth" computer club - list of members

C. Babbage          Loomington      07867-67431            7.50
F. Bilas            Rillingsgate    0189-26265            10.00
G. Boole            Dublin          00353-1-101-10101     10.00
P. Eckert           Ecclestone      0299-211-5678         12.50
L. Frank            Lauder          03929-6611            10.00
R. Freshour         Freshing        06614-333-1212         7.50
H. Goldstine        Washington      0923-2525             12.50
A. Goldstine        Washington      0923-2525              7.50
B. Jennings         Freshing        06614-333-2424         7.50
A. Lovelace         London          071-555-43221          7.50
J. Mauchly          Ecclestone      0299-211-4567         30.00
G. Stibitz          Edinburgh       031-431-2222          15.00
A. Turing           Manchester      061-888111             9.00
J. Weizenbaum       Liverpool       051-666-3333           7.50
J. von Neumann      Southampton     0703-225-6161         10.00

                                             Average: 10.93
                                             Total:  164.00



                Cancel viewing: ESC,  Continue viewing: SPACEBAR
```

In this way you can get a preview of how the printout will be.

☞ Press **Esc** and then any key.

Now you return to the Control Center. Of course, that's no problem.

☞ Press **Enter**, select **Print report** and then **Begin printing** (is the printer switched on?).

Your beautiful list appears:

```
"The Mammoth" computer club - list of members

C. Babbage          Loomington        07867-67431             7.50
F. Bilas            Rillingsgate      0189-26265             10.00
G. Boole            Dublin            00353-1-101-10101      10.00
P. Eckert           Ecclestone        0299-211-5678          12.50
L. Frank            Lauder            03929-6611             10.00
R. Freshour         Freshing          06614-333-1212         7.50
H. Goldstine        Washington        0923-2525              12.50
A. Goldstine        Washington        0923-2525               7.50
B. Jennings         Freshing          06614-333-2424          7.50
A. Lovelace         London            071-555-43221           7.50
J. Mauchly          Ecclestone        0299-211-4567          30.00
G. Stibitz          Edinburgh         031-431-2222           15.00
A. Turing           Manchester        061-888111              9.00
J. Weizenbaum       Liverpool         051-666-3333            7.50
J. von Neumann      Southampton       0703-225-6161          10.00

                                                 Average: 10.93
                                                 Total:  164.00
```

Printing entire records at one time (thus not in columns)

*When designing a report, open the **Layout** menu, select **Quick layout** and then **Form layout**. This option produces a design which prints the data of the entire record at once. This is comparable to the viewing of data in the Edit screen.*

6 Form letters

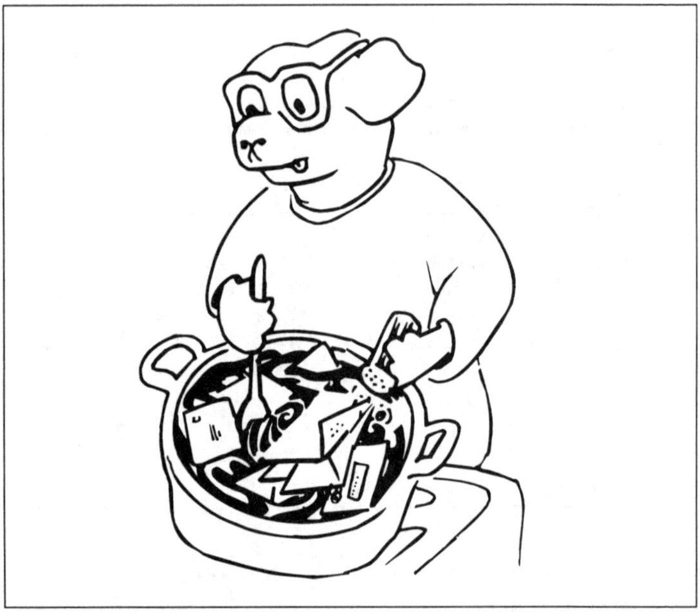

What is a form letter? That is a letter which is sent to a number of people and which has exactly the same text, apart from a few small personal details such as the name and the address for instance. You might receive this kind of letter now and again. It is often an advertisement or special offer containing text like the following:

> Dear Mr/Mrs **EARDRUM**,
>
> There could be celebrations shortly at **34, Walkman Way**. You might be the lucky recipients of a substantial cash prize (up to £150,000)! Simply fill in the enclosed card and send it (no stamp needed) as soon as possible to the address shown. Yes, Mr or Mrs **EARDRUM**, read this card carefully, it could be your passport to .....
>
> *(and so on)*

This letter is sent to many people. The normal text is the same for all receivers, but the personal data such as Mr. or Mrs. **EARDRUM** and **34, Walkman Way** differ from letter to letter. They are taken from a database and are inserted into the letter.

This kind of letter is called a **form letter**.

A form letter for the Mammoth club members

Due to local municipal taxation on computer clubs, the annual contribution has to be increased by £1. Accordingly, two things have to be done.

1. The contribution has to be changed in all the records.
2. The members have to be informed of the changes.

The first point is not difficult. We shall demonstrate just how easy it is to carry out this kind of change in dBASE. This cannot be done using the menus with which we are familiar.

The dot prompt

You can also operate dBASE when you are outside the Control Center. We shall demonstrate this.

- ☞ Ensure you are in the Control Center (you should in fact still be there).
- ☞ Place the marking bar on CLUB and press **Enter**.
- ☞ Select **Close file**.
- ☞ Open the **Exit** menu and select **Exit to dot prompt**. The screen becomes almost completely empty:

The DOT prompt

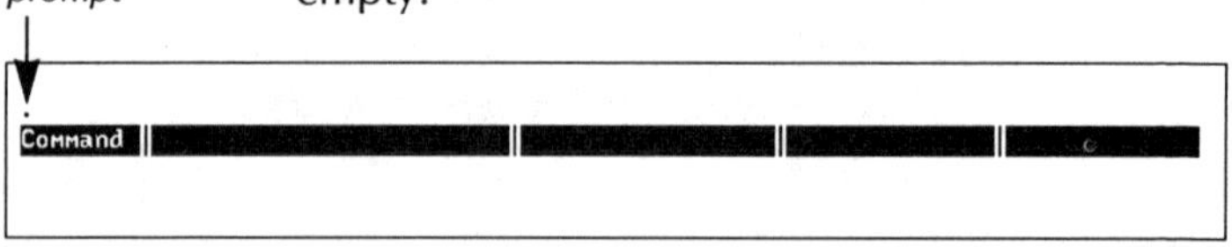

Only the status bar is shown. The word **Command** is displayed at the left. The cursor is flashing behind a dot. This is similar to the DOS prompt **C:\>**. You are able to **type commands** behind this dot prompt. In fact, you can do almost all the things using commands that you can do using menus. For example:

The status bar indicates that no file is currently opened (of course you knew that already).

- ☞ Type **use club** and press **Enter**.

```
. use club
Command
```

Now the CLUB file will be opened, as you will see. We shall browse a little.

☞ Type **browse** and press **Enter**.

The familiar Browse screen appears.

☞ Press **Esc**.

☞ Type **go 6** and press **Enter**.

The status bar indicates that you have moved to record 6.

☞ Type **display surname** and press **Enter**.

The contents of the SURNAME field of record 6 appear on the screen.

```
. go 6
CLUB: Record No       6
. display surname
Record#  surname
     6  Lovelace
.
Command  C:\practice\CLUB      Rec 6/15      File
```

Much more is possible. For instance, you can display the surname, town and the number of diskettes of all the members who possess more than 15 diskettes:

☞ Type **list surname, town, diskettes for diskettes > 15** and press **Enter**.

```
. go 6
CLUB: Record No       6
. display surname
Record#  surname
      6  Lovelace
. list surname, town, diskettes for diskettes >15
Record#  surname            town                diskettes
      2  Boole              Dublin                     20
      3  Goldstine          Washington                 30
      5  Turing             Manchester                 17
      7  Stibitz            Edinburgh                  27
      9  von Neumann        Southampton                17
     12  Eckert             Ecclestone                 25

Command  C:\practice\CLUB      Rec EOF/15      File
```

And you can specify all kinds of conditions or criteria which have to be met. Many of these can also be done by means of the so-called **Queries** which we shall deal with shortly.

There are too many commands to be discussed in this book and we shall not make use of many of them in the rest of this book. If you want to get an idea of the number and kinds of commands you can use, type **help commands** at the dot prompt. Pressing **F4** and **3** will move you through the commands and corresponding information.

Adjusting the contribution automatically

We shall increase the contribution by **£1** in **all** records. We shall have this done **automatically**. We presume that CLUB is still opened. One command will adjust all the records:

☞ Type **replace all contrib with contrib + 1** and press **Enter**.

The following message appears:

```
15 records replaced
```

We shall check if this actually is the case.

☞ Type **browse**. The Browse screen appears.
☞ Press **Ctrl-PgUp** and then **End**.

Yes, it's really true. Compare the printout you made earlier or look at page xxx.

```
Records   Organize   Fields   Go To   Exit
```

POSTCODE	TELEPHONE	BIRTHDATE	DISKETTES	CONTRIB
LM1 1XT	07867-67431	14/05/82	15	8.50
DB7 2ZP	00353-1-101-10101	18/12/82	20	11.00
WS3 5HP	0923-2525	21/04/81	30	13.50
WS3 5HP	0923-2525	12/07/82	10	8.50
MC4 2CL	061-888111	31/01/82	17	10.00
LS 7WW	071-555-43221	03/11/81	12	8.50
EH4 9TH	031-431-2222	11/10/82	27	16.00
LU2 2EU	051-666-3333	19/02/81	11	8.50
SH2 7ED	0703-225-6161	18/05/82	17	11.00
EC1 1EC	0299-211-4567	01/02/81	6	31.00
FR2 1TH	06614-333-1212	03/03/82	15	8.50
EC1 2EC	0299-211-5678	13/01/83	25	13.50
FR3 2JN	06614-333-2424	28/05/83	10	8.50
LD2 5ZD	03929-6611	01/06/81	10	11.00
BG8 2ZEY	0189-26265	29/04/82	15	11.00

```
Browse  C:\practice\CLUB   Rec 1/15   File
```

All contributions have increased by £1

☞ Display the printout of the report design on the screen (press **Esc**, type **assist**, move the marking bar to **NAMES**, press **Enter**, select **Print report** and then **View report on screen**).

You will see here too that the values have been adjusted and that the average and total sums have also been recalculated:

```
Average:     11.93
Total       179.00
```

Press **Esc** twice.

Creating the form letter

We can now begin on the second action which has to be performed concerning the increased contribution. The members have to be notified. We shall create a letter containing a general text; this letter will also contain a few pieces of information which are tailored to that particular member.

If everything has gone properly, you should be in the Control Center and the marking should be on NAMES.

- ☞ Place the marking on **<create>** in the **Reports** panel and press **Enter**.
- ☞ Select **Quick layouts** and then **Mailmerge layout**.

A screen appears, resembling the previous design screen. The way in which it should be filled in is also more or less the same.

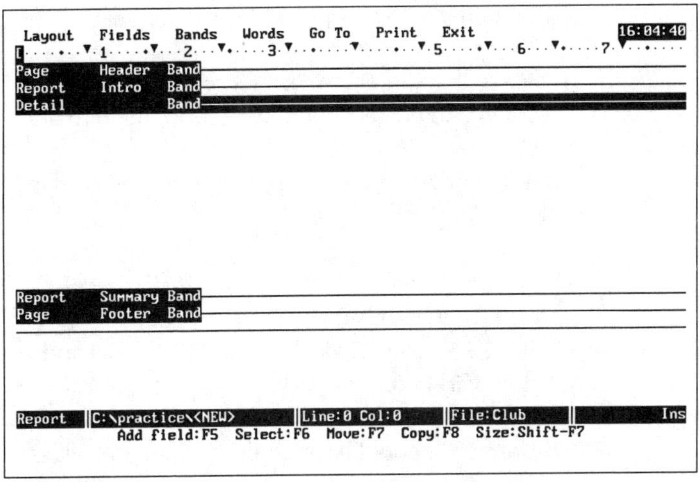

The address data and the date

We shall begin the letter with the name and the address of the club member.

☞ Press **F5** and select **FIRSTNAME**.

We shall again only make use of the first letter of the first name.

☞ Press **Enter** and then ten times on **Backspace**.
☞ Press **Enter** and then **Ctrl-End**.
☞ Type a point behind the X which has been placed on the screen. Then press the spacebar.

Now enter the surname:

☞ Press **F5**, select **SURNAME** and press **Ctrl-End**.

Now do the same for the address data...

☞ Place the address on the second line, and the town and postal code together on the third line.

Then the origin of the letter and the date should be displayed:

☞ Leave two empty lines and then type **Silicon Hill**. Then type a comma and a space.
☞ Press **F5**, select **Date** from the third panel and then **Ctrl-End**.

Of course we could have typed the date ourselves; but the advantage of doing it this way is that the current date is placed in the letter automatically, regardless of when we print the letter. Thus, the letter is never out-of-date.

The actual letter

☞ Skip another line and type **Dear** followed by a space.

A template for the first name should be placed behind this intro. A comma should follow, but this presents us with a problem. For instance, in the letter to Ada Lovelace, the first line would be:

```
Dear Ada
```

Now there is a lot of space between the name and the comma. You might say, OK shorten the name to three letters. But what about the letter to Charles Babbage?

```
Dear Cha,
```

Fortunately, dBASE is aware of this problem. When we place the template, we can determine whether or not spaces which might occur are to be omitted. Thus, any data following the template shifts to fit the length of the field **without** spaces. In that case, we get:

```
Dear Ada,
```

and also:

```
Dear Charles,
```

This is the standard setting in form letters. Have a good look:

☞ Press **F5** and select **FIRSTNAME**. The familiar box appears, showing 'Template' among other things. Select **Picture functions**.

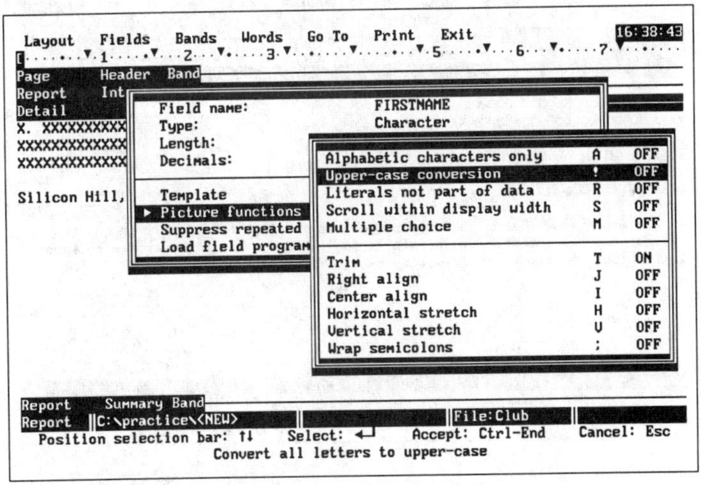

☞ Move the marking to **Trim**. The Help line shows:

```
Remove all leading and trailing blanks
```

Behind the word **Trim**, a **T** is shown and also the word **ON**. This means that this possibility is activated. This means you do not have to do anything special. However, keep this in mind: it might be useful in other situations.

☞ Press **Esc** and then **Ctrl-End**.
☞ Press the → cursor key and then a comma. Then press **Enter** twice.
☞ Now type the following (you create the pound sign by pressing and holding down the Alt key and typing 156 on the numeric pad at the right of your keyboard; then release the Alt key), pressing Enter when you reach the end of the line:

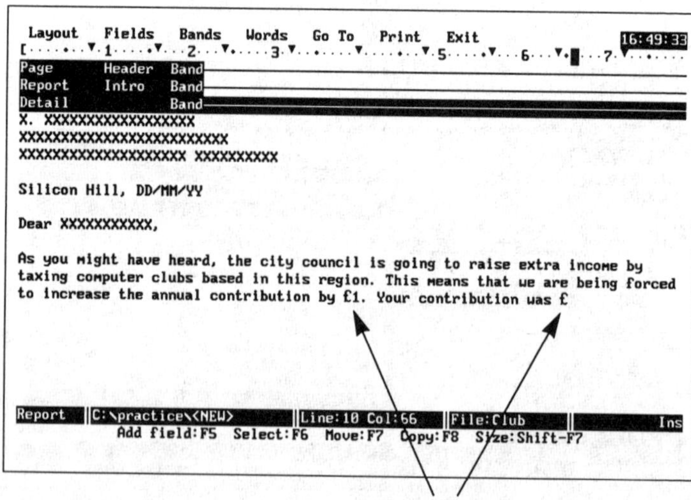

Alt-156

A Calculated field

What should we do now? We want to display the **previous** contribution at this position, thus, the current contribution minus one. We can do this by means of a template for a **calculated field**. This does not mean that we have to add a new field to the database, only that we have to create a temporary field which only exists in the report design. The contents of the field are **calculated** by means of a formula which we enter in the template.

This is done as follows:

☞ Press **F5**.
☞ Select **<create>** in the **CALCULATED** panel.

The familiar box appears once more, but this time we have to fill in a number of things ourselves.

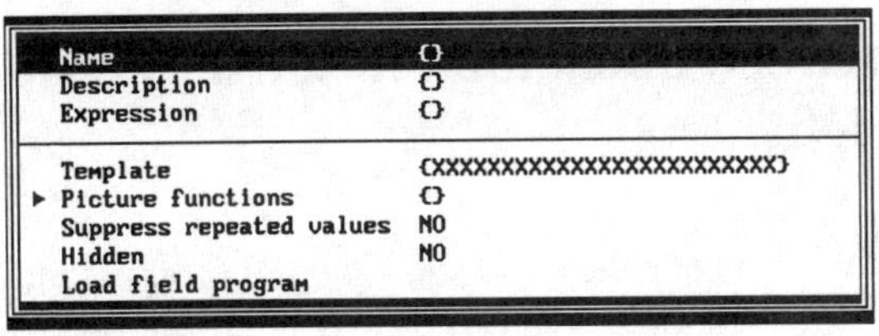

☞ Select **Name** and type **oldcontrb**. Then press **Enter**.

Then we have to specify what has to be placed in the Calculated field. That is the contents of the CONTRIB field minus one.

☞ Select **Expression**. You can use Shift-F1 to help

you choose a field, but you can simply type the name as well. Type **contrib-1** and press **Enter**.

dBASE knows immediately that you are working with the CONTRIB field and changes the Template correspondingly to nines (it is after all a **numeric** field). We shall shorten this template a little.

☞ Select **Template** and remove the first five nines. Then press **Enter**.

You will see that a **T** is again displayed alongside the **Picture functions**. This means, as we mentioned above, that the **Trim** function is active.

☞ Press **Ctrl-End**.

The Calculated field is shown on the screen.

Having a quick look to see if everything's alright

Let's look and see if we are progressing as we should. We can display the result on screen as you already know.

☞ Open the **Print** menu and select **View report on screen**.

```
C. Babbage
1 Mill Lane
Loomington LM1 1XT

Silicon Hill, 18/10/94

Dear Charles,

As you might have heard, the city council is going to raise extra income by
taxing computer clubs based in this region. This means that we are being forced
to increase the annual contribution by £1. Your contribution was £7.50
```

This is the calculated field

Well, this looks fine.

☞ Press **Esc** twice. You now return to the design screen.

☞ Type a full stop behind the Calculated field template. Then type **It will now become £** and place a template for the CONTRIB field. You will know how to do this by now.

☞ Then type a full stop and a space.

Another Calculated field

We shall add another Calculated field. We shall state, just to round things off, whether this member pays **more** or **less** than the average contribution. This calculation is also not difficult.

☞ Type: **It is perhaps interesting to know that you now pay**

☞ Then type a space and press **F5**. Select **<create>** in the **CALCULATED** panel.

☞ Select **Expression**. We know from our previous list that the average contribution is **£12.93** (£11.93+1). Now type **iif(contrib<12.93,"less","more")** and press **Enter**.

This is one of the many functions provided by dBASE. You don't need to remember it, but the rather strange term **iif** stands for *immediate if.* It is in fact a kind of condition formula meaning: 'If the contents of the CONTRIB field are less than £12.93, apply the word **less** and if the contents are greater, apply the word **more**.

- ☞ Reduce the template to four Xs and press **Ctrl-End**.
- ☞ Type a space and then the words **than the average contribution**.
- ☞ Place the cursor on the Calculated field. We have not given this field a name as yet, but the Help line shows the formula we have used.
- ☞ Complete the letter as shown in the figure below.

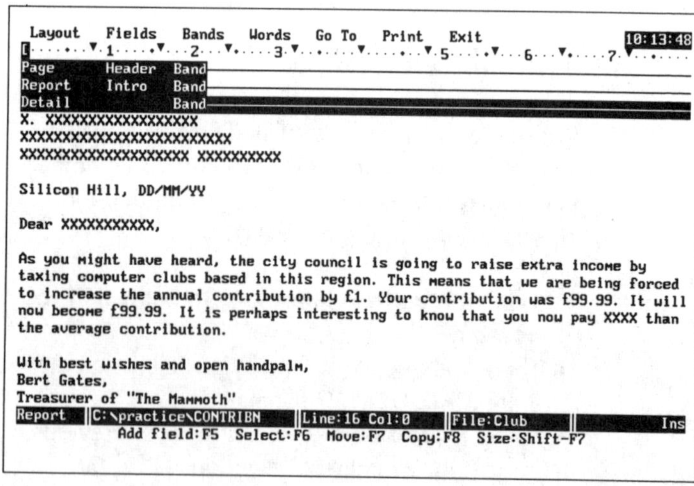

The final merge

The time has finally arrived to print the form letters. We shall first save the model letter.

- ☞ Open the **Print** menu and select **Save settings to print form**.
- ☞ Assign the name **formix**.
- ☞ Ensure that there is paper in the printer.
- ☞ Select **Begin printing** from the **Print** menu.

If everything has gone smoothly, you should now get 15 letters. We display two of them here, just to let you see how they look.

```
C. Babbage
1 Mill Lane
Loomington LM1 1XT


Silicon Hill, 18/10/94

Dear Charles,

As you might have heard, the city council is going to raise extra income
by taxing computer clubs based in this region. This means that we are
being forced to increase the annual contribution by £1. Your contribution
was £7.50. It will now become £8.50. It is perhaps interesting to know
that you now pay less than the average contribution.

With best wishes and open handpalm,

Bert Gates,
Treasurer of "The Mammoth"
```

First calculated field — *Second calculated field* — *The CONTRIB field*

```
G. Boole
22 Algebra Avenue
Dublin DB7 22P


Silicon Hill, 18/10/94

Dear George,

As you might have heard, the city council is going to raise extra income
by taxing computer clubs based in this region. This means that we are
being forced to increase the annual contribution by £1. Your contribution
was £10.00. It will now become £11.00. It is perhaps interesting to know
that you now pay less than the average contribution.

With best wishes and open handpalm,

Bert Gates,
Treasurer of "The Mammoth"
```

Labels

We are not completely finished with our letters. Names and addresses have to be placed on the envelopes. The most attractive method is to use window envelopes so that the part of the letter containing the name and address can be seen through the transparent section. We could also write the names and addresses by hand. Some printers are able to print on envelopes. Another (increasingly) common practice is to print names and addresses on labels.

The last two options mentioned can be done by means of the **Labels** panel in the Control Center. We shall discuss this briefly.

We shall leave the form letter screen.

- ☞ Press **Esc** and answer **Y** to the question which appears.
- ☞ Move the marking bar to **<create>** in the **Labels** panel and press **Enter**. The following screen appears:

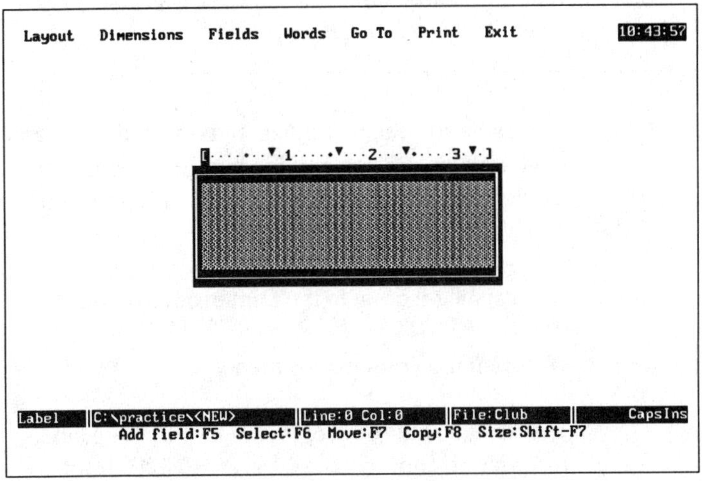

How big are the labels?

This rectangle in the middle of the screen represents a label. The problem is that you have to specify very precisely how large the labels (or envelopes) are that you want to use.

Look at the wrapping!

The packaging containing the labels (or envelopes) often indicate their size. If you have thrown it away, you will have to get the measuring tape out. You can of course just apply the well-known 'trial-and-error' method.

You can also specify the size in terms of the number of characters per line and the number of lines per label. Here, dBASE uses 'Pica' units (also referred to as 10 cpi: 10 characters per inch).

This can all be done in the **Dimensions** menu.

☞ Open the **Dimensions** menu.

The default setting accepts sheets with three labels next to one another. The labels are 15/16ths of an inch by 3½ inches. You can change this according to your own needs. If you want to check if you have chosen the right size, you can open the **Print** menu and select **Generate sample labels**. Then labels are printed with only Xs, such as:

```
xxxxxxxxxxxxxxxxxxxxxxxxxxxxxxxxxxx
xxxxxxxxxxxxxxxxxxxxxxxxxxxxxxxxxxx
xxxxxxxxxxxxxxxxxxxxxxxxxxxxxxxxxxx
xxxxxxxxxxxxxxxxxxxxxxxxxxxxxxxxxxx
xxxxxxxxxxxxxxxxxxxxxxxxxxxxxxxxxxx
```

In this way, you can see if your settings fit.

When you have the proper size, you can begin to place the field templates, just as you did with the column layout and the form letters.

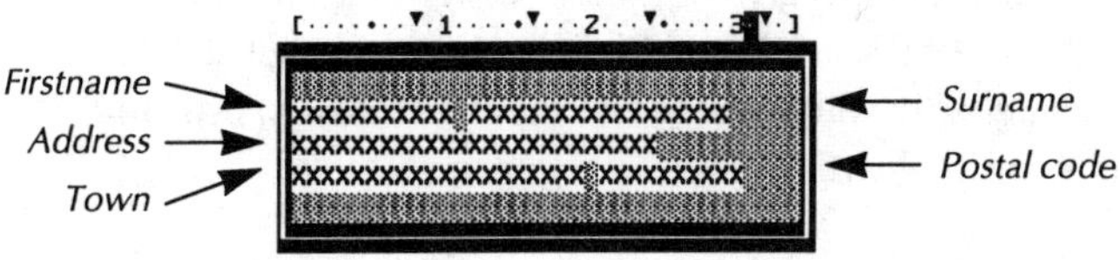

If everything has gone well, the labels will roll neatly out of the printer:

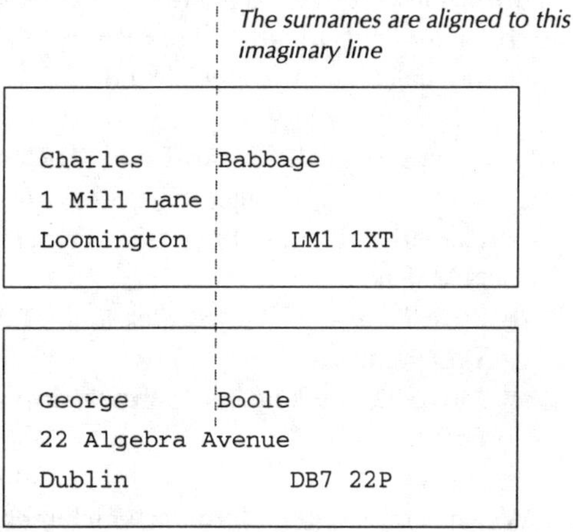

But wait a minute, why aren't the surnames next to the first names? As you will have seen, the 'Trim' function was activated. This is because the surname has been placed at a **fixed position**. This means that other settings are simply ignored!

Getting rid of superfluous spaces

Fortunately, there is a solution to this problem. And this will also give you more insight into the possibilities of dBASE. We shall again use a CALCULATED field, this time **instead** of the fields SURNAME and FIRSTNAME.

"A Calculated field?" you might exclaim. "How can you calculate with character fields?" Of course, you're right, it's not possible to **add up** two words. But what we can do is **paste** the contents of two character fields together. For dBASE, this is also a kind of calculation, a special kind.

☞ Remove the **FIRSTNAME** and **SURNAME** fields from the label design (mark them and press **Del**).
☞ Place the cursor at the position where the FIRSTNAME field began.
☞ Press **F5** and select **<create>** in the **CALCULATED** panel.
☞ Move the marking bar to **Expression** and press **Enter**.

We shall now enter a formula which means the following: 'Place the contents of the FIRSTNAME field here **without** the superfluous spaces; place one space behind the first name and then place the SURNAME field behind this.'

☞ Type **trim(firstname)+" "+surname** and press **Enter**.
☞ Select **Template** and increase the size of the template by typing a number of Xs. This should be sufficient.

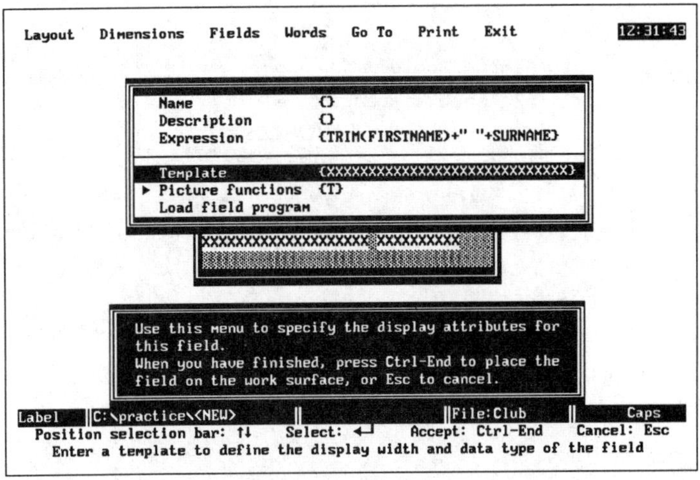

☞ Press **Ctrl-End**.

The design now clearly shows that the first line consists of one field.

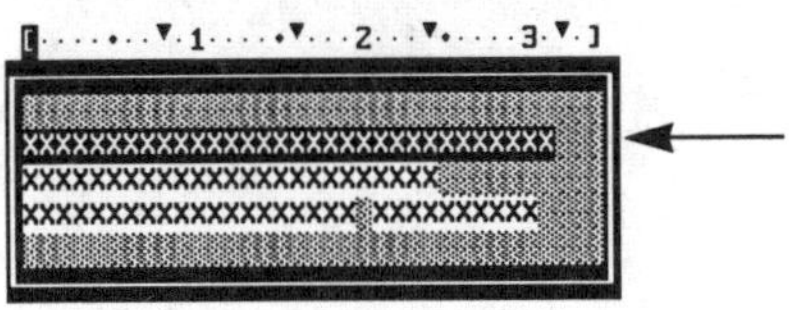

This is one field

If you now try printing again, it will look just as you want it to be.

```
Charles Babbage
1 Mill Lane
Loomington        LM1 1XT
```

```
George Boole
22 Algebra Avenue
Dublin            DB7 22P
```

You can, of course, print envelopes instead of labels (if your printer can perform this task).

You can save the label design, just like other print designs.

7 Linking files

In this last chapter, we shall illustrate how you can link files in dBASE. It is not difficult, although it might seem complicated. In fact, you can regard this chapter as a small demonstration of the extensive possibilities available in dBASE.

Queries

You have probably already noticed the **Queries** panel in the Control Center. A **Query** enables you to use all kinds of conditions or criteria or **filters** to **examine** data. For instance, you can ask to be shown the records of only those members who live in Washington. This is a criterion. You can also **link** data by means of this panel.

A query is **not** a new file. In a query, certain data from one or more files are **selected** and displayed on the screen. In fact, it is a special way of examining data.

We shall link the data from two files by means of a query. Of course, we need a second file. We shall create this.

Another file

Imagine that the treasurer wants to keep track of all the computer programs the club members possess. This is convenient, because the members can borrow the various programs from one another. You could create a new field in the CLUB file to contain this information, but that is not very suitable since some members may have as many as 20 computer programs.

For this reason, the treasurer has come up with a different idea. He creates another database with only **two** fields: one with the membership number and one with the name of the computer program. If a member acquires or writes a new program, he/she sends a letter to the treasurer. The treasurer then enters the membership number and the name of the computer program in the new database. Thus, the membership numbers will probably occur several times in this database. For example, there may be ten records with membership number 8; the name of the computer program will be different each time.

On the one hand, this is very convenient since each membership number is unique: no two membership numbers are alike, and if you know someone's membership number you can always look up the name and address it belongs to. But on the other hand, this can be a bit troublesome, because you have to actually look up the name and address in another file when you want to borrow a computer program. You could solve the problem by entering the name and address in each record in the new database, but that costs you a lot of typework and mistakes are also easily made.

Linking

You can solve this problem by linking the files. They are linked by means of the field containing the membership number. Then you can examine the data in both files simultaneously. Of course, we don't need to examine all the data in both files: if one member wants to borrow a program from another, it is not important how much contribution he/she pays. But the name, address and telephone number **are** important.

Let's see if we can organise all this. We shall begin by creating a new file. We shall call it CLUBSOFT.

There are two important points here:

1. The field through which we want to make the link, the field with the membership number, has to be the same type of field in both files. In this case, it will have to be a character field. The

names do not need to be identical. The field lengths may also differ as long as the **data** contained are of the same length.

2. We have to index on the field through which we want to create the link. This is not absolutely necessary but it makes working with the link much more convenient.

Creating the CLUBSOFT file

- ☞ Ensure that you are in the dBASE Control Center.
- ☞ Select **<create>** in in the **Data** panel.
- ☞ Fill in the structure of the new database as shown in the figure below:

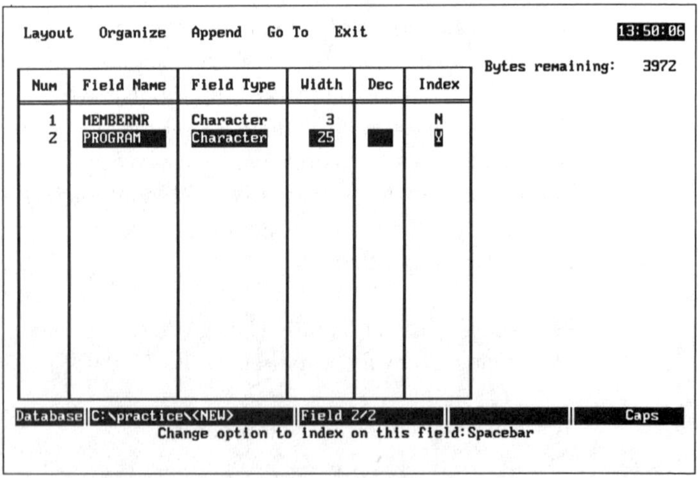

Have a good look at the **Index** column. We have placed a **Y** there. This means that an index will be made on this field automatically. This will be very convenient. The index is **not** automatically activated when you open the file. This index will not be used in the linking.

☞ When you have created the database as shown, press **Ctrl-End** and specify the name **CLUBSOFT**.
☞ Answer **N** to the question **Input data records now?**.

Entering some data

Imagine that a number of letters have already arrived from members who want to register their programs. We shall use this information to fill in the database, in the same order of sequence as the letters arrived. Attention: there must be **no active index** when we are doing this.

The procedure is as follows (the file is opened as you can see in the Control Center).

☞ Press **F2**.
☞ Enter MEMBERNR **003**, and the program **Larry 1**.
☞ Press **Enter**, select **Yes** to enter more records and then press **F2**. You are now in the Browse screen and you can use the ↓ cursor key to move to the next record.

The final result should look something like this:

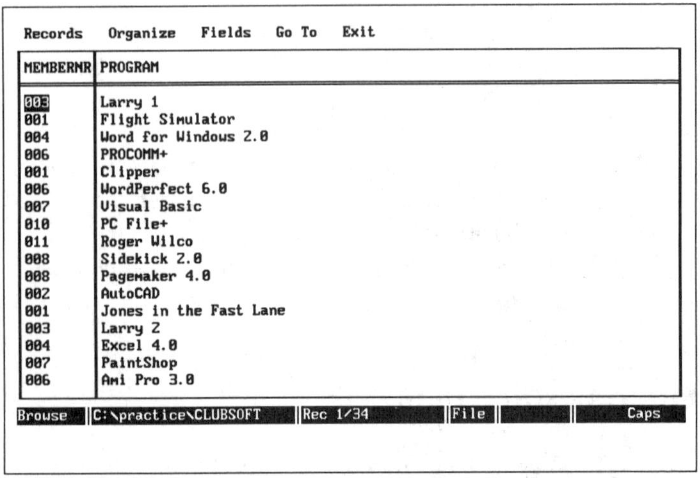

There are several programs which are doubly mentioned, but that is not so surprising. The members do not know exactly what the others are interested in buying (if that were the case, this database would not be necessary!).

As you see, the information is available but you do not know who is actually the owner of which program.

On to the Query

It is not easy to quickly describe exactly what a query is or does. You could regard it as being a kind of filter or pair of spectacles through which only the chosen data can be seen. All other data are excluded. It is not a file, it is only a **way of looking** at data in file(s). If the data change, the query itself does not change; but only the data which satisfy the conditions of the query will be shown.

We shall create a query. First, we shall illustrate the structure using one file, CLUB.

☞ Go back to the Control Center (press Esc) and open the **CLUB** file.

☞ Move the marking bar to **<create>** in the **Queries** panel and press **Enter**.

This screen is displayed:

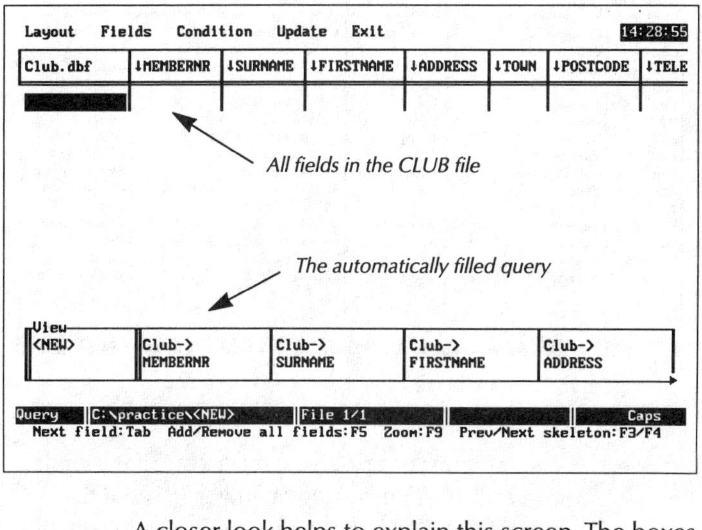

A closer look helps to explain this screen. The boxes at the top of the screen indicate that we are working with the CLUB file; all the field names are shown along with arrows pointing downwards. At the bottom of the screen, there are boxes showing:

```
Club->
```

with a field name underneath.

The boxes at the bottom represent the contents of the query. This query has already been made automatically, and all the fields in the opened file (CLUB) have been automatically included. This is always the case if you create a query with an opened file.

☞ Press **F2**.

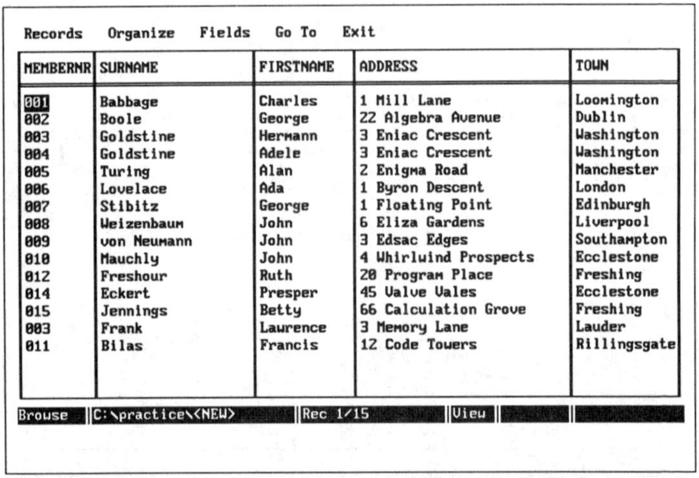

You are presented with a familiar list. That is both true and not true. What you now see is not the normal CLUB **file**, it is the new **query** in which **all** the fields in the CLUB file have been included. In this case, the filter is not strict at all.

Now look at the status bar. The word **View** is shown there.

Just as everyone has his/her own point of view about matters like whether a teacher gives good or bad lessons or a certain popgroup churns out good music or rubbish, you can also develop your own view (or filter) with regard to one or more files in dBASE. In this case, 'Query' and 'View' mean more or less the same.

Complicated?

This seems rather vague but you will shortly see exactly what the difference is between the View and the normal file.

We shall repeat what we said earlier: A query is **not** a new file. In a query, certain data are **selected** from one or more files and displayed on the screen. It is a special way of **examining** data.

☞ Open the **Exit** menu and select **Transfer to Query Design**.
☞ Press **F5**. This empties the query in a single stroke.

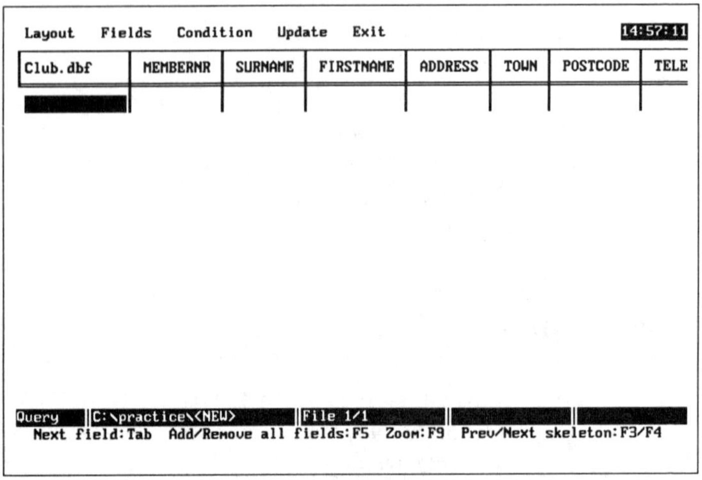

The boxes at the bottom of the screen have disappeared and the arrows pointing downwards in the upper boxes have also gone. You can switch between adding and removing all the fields in the query by pressing F5 (see the Help line). Try this out a few times.

Our own query

We shall now create our own query. In this we want to see the following data: the surname, the town, the number of diskettes and the dates of birth of the club members who possess more than **12** diskettes. This is done as follows:

☞ Press the **Tab** key twice. The marking is then on the **SURNAME** field.

☞ Press **F5**.

Do you see what is happening? A new query is being created, in which the **SURNAME** field from the **CLUB** file is included. This is shown by:

If you examine the boxes at the top of the screen, you will see that the SURNAME field has an arrow pointing downwards.

☞ Press **F2** again. You will see that only the surnames are displayed:

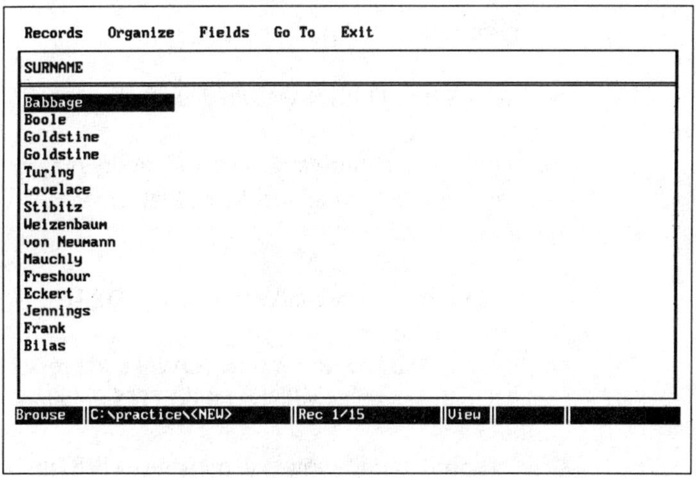

☞ Press **Shift-F2**. You return to the Query design screen.

You can move from one field to the other by pressing **Tab** and **Shift-Tab**. By pressing **F3** and **F4** you can move from the CLUB boxes at the top to the query boxes at the bottom and back again.

☞ Press **Tab** and then **F5**. The **FIRSTNAME** field has now been included in the query. Check this by pressing **F2**. You can return by pressing **Shift-F2**.

But this was not our intention! No panic.

☞ Press **F4** and then **Tab**. The marking is now on the third box at the bottom:

```
Club->
FIRSTNAME
```

☞ Press **F5**. The FIRSTNAME field jumps back!

This is quite straightforward. Well, the theory may be complicated, the practice shows that it's only a matter of routine.

☞ Press **F4** again. The marking is now at **FIRSTNAME** at the top.
☞ Press the **Tab** key to move to **TOWN** and press **F5**. Do the same to add the **DISKETTES** field to the query.
☞ Press **Shift-Tab** to move the marking to **BIRTHDATE** and press **F5**.

The result should look like this:

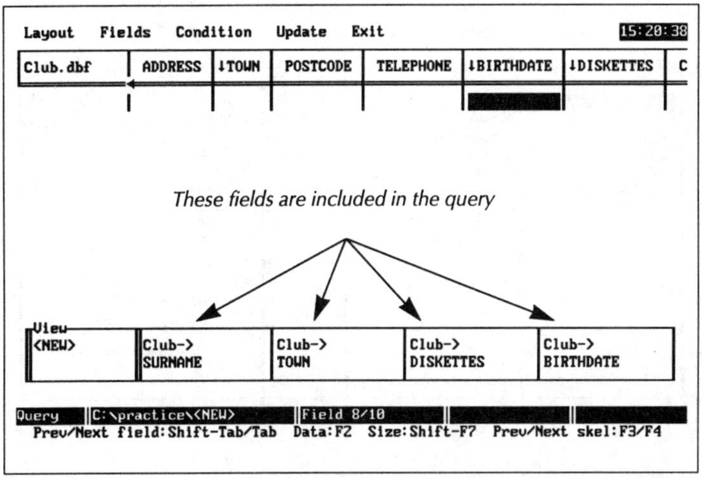

Now we want to define the query so that only the members who have more than 12 diskettes will be displayed.

☞ Open the **Condition** menu and select **Add condition box**.

A condition box appears on the screen.

☞ Type **diskettes>12** here. (You can also use Shift-F1 to help you.)

You can quit this box by pressing F4 or F3.

☞ Press **F2**. The result is perfect.

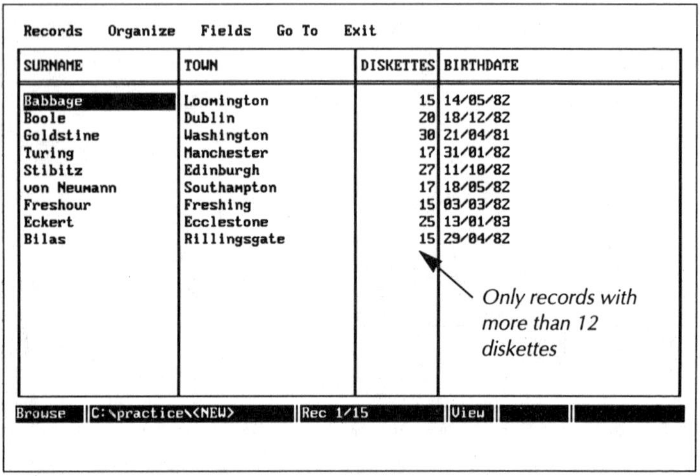

We repeat: you have not created a new file, only a **filter** which enables you to examine data in a particular way. We can also save this filter so that we can use it later when we want.

☞ First press **Shift-F2** and open the **Exit** menu. Select **Save changes and exit**. Specify the name **disk12**.

The **DISK12** query is shown in the **Queries** panel. The handy thing is that you can simply open this query as if it were a file. You will see that the CLUB file is not opened (the name is under the line), but if you open DISK12, the data from CLUB becomes automatically available. You can use F2 to examine the data directly as you would normally do. The useful part of this is that if you change the data in the CLUB file (for instance Charles Babbage's father wins the pools and gives Charles £10,000 to buy diskettes), the query will show this alteration.

You can also look through, alter and delete the data in a query. But be careful. We shall outline how to protect your data against deletion a little further on in this chapter.

Finally making the link

☞ Ensure that **no** file is opened. If a file is opened, place the marking on it and press Enter twice.
☞ Select **<create>** from the **Query** panel.

The screen looks more empty than on the previous occasion. This is because no file was opened. A menu is automatically opened.

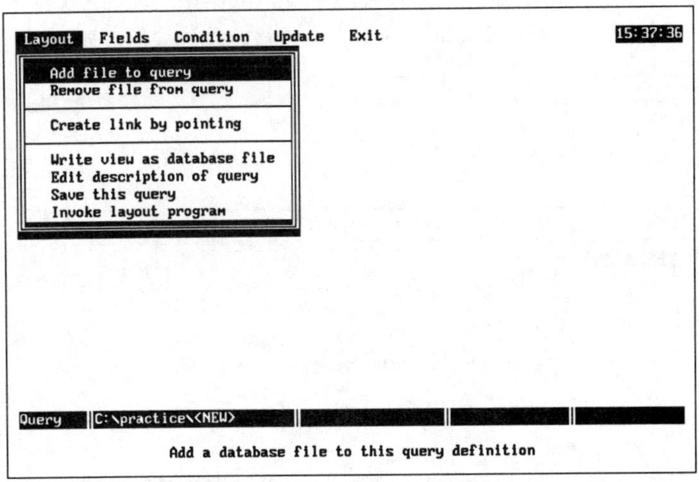

We want to be able to gain access to data in two files. Our query, which is a special way of looking at data in files, is going to make use of certain fields in the files we created, CLUBSOFT and CLUB.

☞ Select the first option, **Add file to query**.

☞ Select **CLUBSOFT.DBF** (remember to press **Enter**).

☞ Now open the **Layout** menu again and select **Add file to query** once more.

☞ Select **CLUB.DBF**.

You now have two files available from which you can adopt fields into the query.

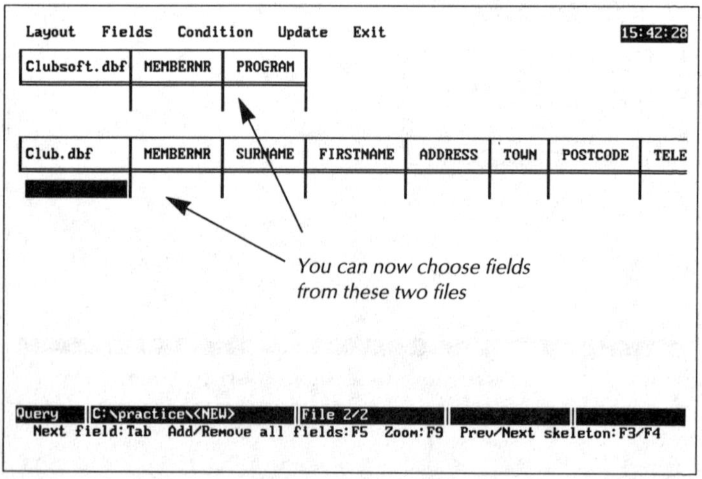

☞ Press **F4** to move to the **CLUBSOFT** structure.
☞ Press **Tab** twice and then **F5**. The **PROGRAM** field is added to the query.

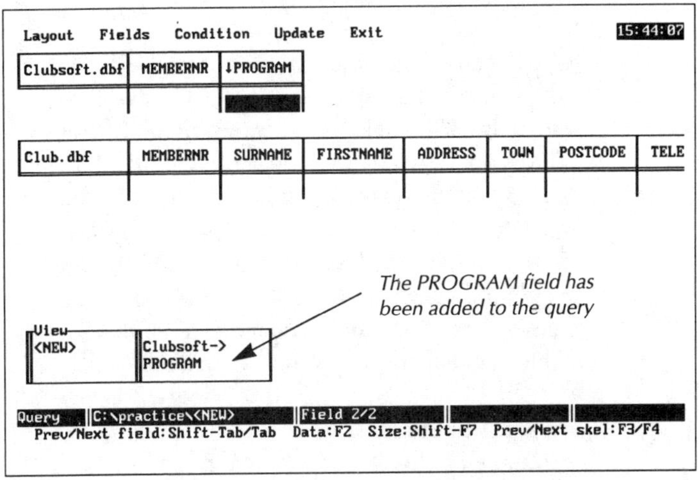

Now we shall choose two fields from the **CLUB** file. We actually only need the first name, the surname and the telephone number. The members can telephone one another to ask if the desired program can be borrowed.

☞ Press **F4** to move to the **CLUB** structure.
☞ Place the marking on **FIRSTNAME** and press **F5**.
☞ Press **Shift-Tab** to go to the **SURNAME** field and press **F5**.
☞ Include the **TELEPHONE** field in the query in the same way.

Don't imagine that the link has already been made; that would be a mistake. Press F2 to examine the data. The following error message appears:

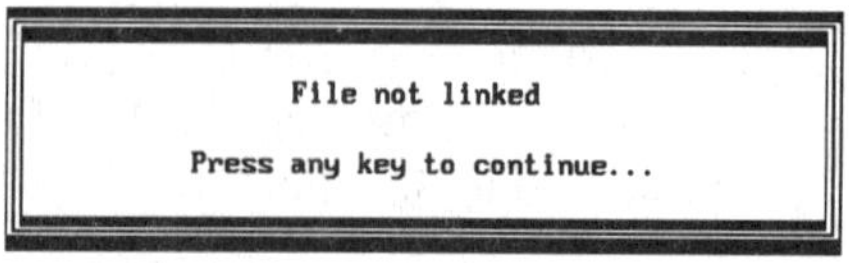

We have to indicate that we want to link the files. The link is to be made via the MEMBERNR field since this is the field that is **common** to both files. This is done by going to the MEMBERNR field in the CLUB structure and typing one word. Then you have to go to the MEMBERNR field in the CLUB-SOFT structure and type the **same word**. It makes no difference which word that is, but it must be the same word. This is how you indicate to dBASE which fields you want to use to make the link.

- ☞ Press **Shift-Tab** to go to MEMBERNR in CLUB and type **link**.
- ☞ Press **F4** twice to go to the CLUBSOFT structure. Press **Shift-Tab** to go to MEMBERNR and type **link** there too.

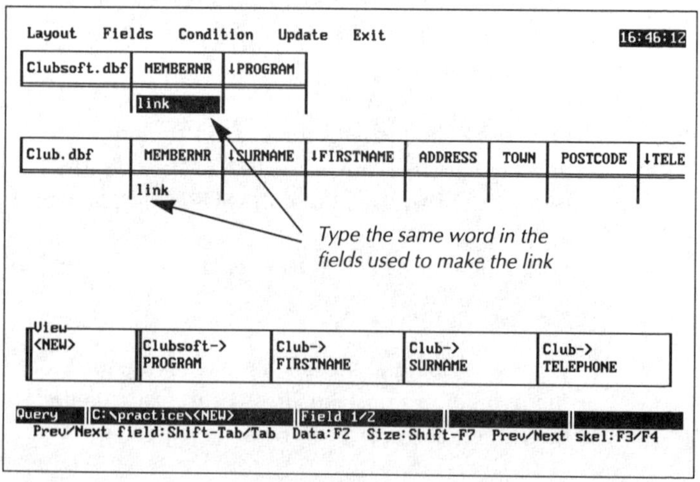

☞ Now press **F2**!

```
Records   Organize   Fields   Go To   Exit
```

PROGRAM	FIRSTNAME	SURNAME	TELEPHONE
Larry 1	Hermann	Goldstine	0923-2525
Larry 1	Laurence	Frank	03929-6611
Flight Simulator	Charles	Babbage	07867-67431
Word for Windows 2.0	Adele	Goldstine	0923-2525
PROCOMM+	Ada	Lovelace	071-555-43221
Clipper	Charles	Babbage	07867-67431
WordPerfect 6.0	Ada	Lovelace	071-555-43221
Visual Basic	George	Stibitz	031-431-2222
PC File+	John	Mauchly	0299-211-4567
Roger Wilco	Francis	Bilas	0189-26265
Sidekick 2.0	John	Weizenbaum	051-666-3333
Pagemaker 4.0	John	Weizenbaum	051-666-3333
AutoCAD	George	Boole	00353-1-101-10101
Jones in the Fast Lane	Charles	Babbage	07867-67431
Larry 2	Hermann	Goldstine	0923-2525
Larry 2	Laurence	Frank	03929-6611
Excel 4.0	Adele	Goldstine	0923-2525

```
Browse  C:\practice\<NEW>   Rec 1/34   View
```

The link is successful but the result is rather disorganised. We must do something about that.

☞ Press **Shift-F2**.

☞ Press **Tab** (the marking should now be on PROGRAM) and open the **Fields** menu.

☞ Select **Sort on this field**.

☞ An options window appears. Select **Ascending Dictionary**.

```
Ascending  ASCII       (0-9..A-Z..a-z)
Descending ASCII       (z-a..Z-A..9-0)

Ascending  Dictionary  (0-9..Aa-Zz)
Descending Dictionary  (zZ-aA..9-0)
```

☞ Press **F4** to go to the CLUB structure and do the same to the SURNAME and FIRSTNAME fields.

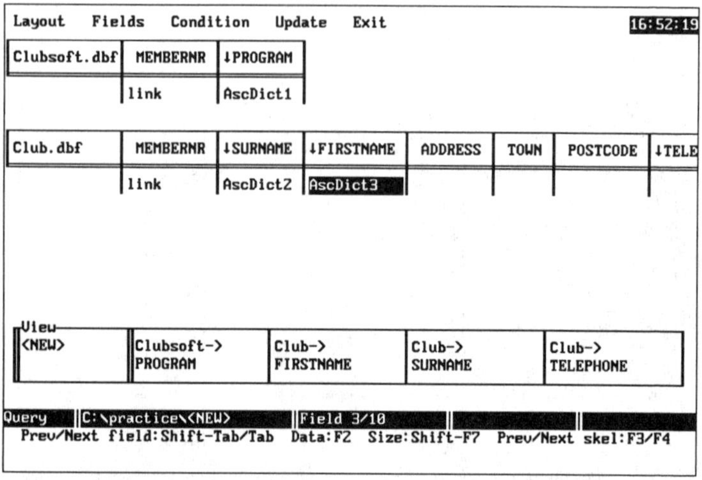

The data - Read Only

Now we have to do something quite important. We do not want anything in the query to be altered when the data are being examined. Normally, it is possible to change the data if you are browsing through. But we feel that this might lead to confusion. The data in the original files may be altered (programs come and go) but the query should remain as it is. For this reason, we shall protect the fields in the query so that the data shown there become **read only** data.

- Press **F4** to go to the query structure at the bottom of the screen. The marking bar is positioned at 'Clubsoft->PROGRAM'.
- Press **F8**.

The letters **R/O** appear at the bottom of this box. This means 'Read Only'. The F8 key is a kind of switch. You can use it to switch 'Read Only' on and off.

☞ Do the same to the other four fields in the query (**Tab**, **F8** etc.).
☞ Then press **F2** to examine the data.

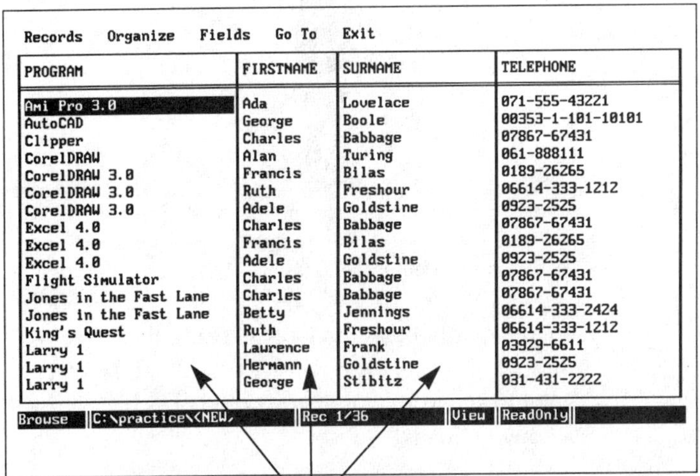

Records   Organize   Fields   Go To   Exit

PROGRAM	FIRSTNAME	SURNAME	TELEPHONE
Ami Pro 3.0	Ada	Lovelace	071-555-43221
AutoCAD	George	Boole	00353-1-101-10101
Clipper	Charles	Babbage	07867-67431
CorelDRAW	Alan	Turing	061-888111
CorelDRAW 3.0	Francis	Bilas	0189-26265
CorelDRAW 3.0	Ruth	Freshour	06614-333-1212
CorelDRAW 3.0	Adele	Goldstine	0923-2525
Excel 4.0	Charles	Babbage	07867-67431
Excel 4.0	Francis	Bilas	0189-26265
Excel 4.0	Adele	Goldstine	0923-2525
Flight Simulator	Charles	Babbage	07867-67431
Jones in the Fast Lane	Charles	Babbage	07867-67431
Jones in the Fast Lane	Betty	Jennings	06614-333-2424
King's Quest	Ruth	Freshour	06614-333-1212
Larry 1	Laurence	Frank	03929-6611
Larry 1	Hermann	Goldstine	0923-2525
Larry 1	George	Stibitz	031-431-2222

Browse | C:\practice\<NEW> | Rec 1/36 | View | ReadOnly

Sorted according to PROGRAM, SURNAME and FIRSTNAME

That's more like it, don't you think?

Of course we have to save this query.

☞ Press **Shift-F2** to return to the query design.
☞ Open the **Layout** menu and select **Save this query**.
☞ Assign the name **findsoft.**

You will notice that you are only able to read the data; you cannot alter them. The status bar shows 'ReadOnly'.

Bodybuilders demand education

Searching (that was the whole idea of the exercise) through the query is now very easy. Imagine you want to see from whom you could possibly borrow a copy of 'Space Quest':

- ☞ Place the marking in the **PROGRAM** field.
- ☞ Open the **Go To** menu and select **Forwards search**. Specify **Space Quest** (wildcards work here too).

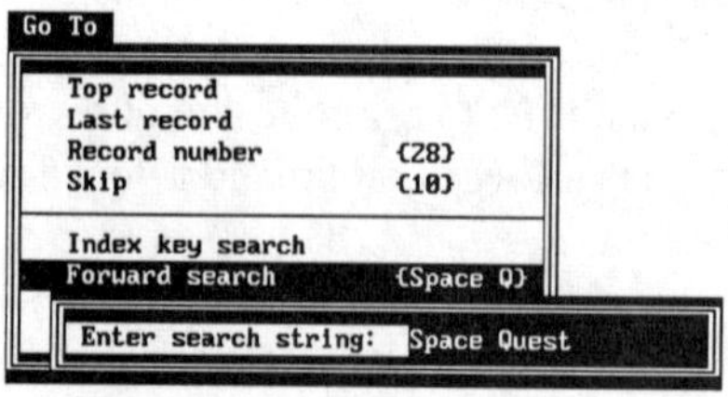

It works great!

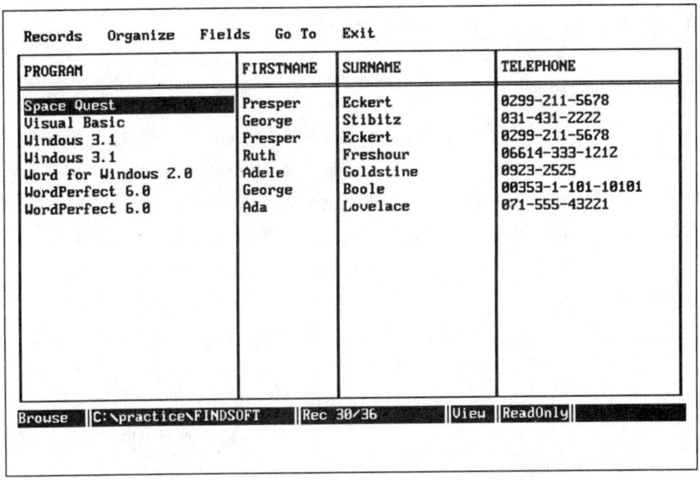

In the future, you only need to open this query and then press F2 to be able to examine these data. And, as we mentioned, if you add or change data in the relevant fields in the CLUB or CLUBSOFT files, this will be shown in the query.

Saving the query as a database file

You can also save the query as a ***database file****. All the data are then automatically copied to a new file. dBASE creates the structure for this itself. Keep in mind that this is a* ***new file****, independent of the files which you used to create the query. There is no longer a link to those other files. Thus, changes in one of the original files are no longer passed on to the new file. If you want to create this new file, open the* ***Layout*** *menu in the query design screen and select* ***Write view as database file****. A little experimenting will do no harm if you have saved the query already.*

Thinking about linking

Have you realised that the field which is used to **make the link** (MEMBERNR in our case) does not need to be included in the query? In fact, this is very convenient because displaying the membership number is of no use to us. We only need names, programs and telephone numbers in this case.

Keep in mind that the data in the linking field have to be **unique**: in other words (in our example), no two membership numbers may be alike. For this reason, a link according to surname would not work.

Deliberation about location

You now have a lot of files in the PRACTICE directory. You will be aware of the fact that these files are largely related to one another. If, for instance, you were to move the CLUBSOFT file to a different directory, the FINDSOFT query would no longer work, because one of the sources of data has gone. Remember this when you are deleting or removing files.

The end

We have come to the end of this book. Of course, dBASE is so extensive that we have not been able to discuss all of its far-reaching facilities. But don't be afraid to experiment yourself with fields, records and files. As long as you save your work regularly, you will always have a backup copy if anything should go wrong.

In addition, it is also possible to write your own **computer programs** in dBASE. dBASE provides much support and assistance for this and the results can be quite satisfying. That is perhaps a topic for the next book ...

Index

PRISMA

be an expert

also in this series:

Programming with QBasic

be an expert!

If you want the computer to carry out your own special wishes, you have to program it. This means that you create a list of commands which the computer has to perform. Of course, you must do this according to particular rules, in a certain language. The language we deal with in this book is called QBasic. When you get your computer, you are also supplied with QBasic. Programming in this language can be done quickly and easily. The results of your work are immediately obvious.
When you have finished this book, you will not only be able to write your own programs, you will have also created the following programs:

- a program to make your computer beep
- a program to capture hearts
- a program to play the game of Mastermind
- a program to arrange the sports results
- a program to keep track of your pocket money and to write menus
- a program for making tunes.

There is something for everybody. There's a whole world just waiting to be programmed!

ISBN 1-85365-346-2

PRISMA *be an* expert

also in this series:

Word Processing with WordPerfect

be an expert!

Everybody wants to work with WordPerfect. But... how do you go about it? If you use this book, you can find out how WordPerfect enables you to apply all kinds of word processing features. For instance you can write your text in columns just as in newspapers or magazines, you can move whole passages of text, you can even place drawings in your letters and documents.

It does not matter if you have not used this program before - everything will be explained right from the very beginning. And when you have finished this book, you will be ready to step into the world of Fleet Street!

Some of the exercises in this book:

- making an invitation to a party
- changing the appearance of the letters (bold, italics, underlined, size, spacing etc.)
- using the automatic spelling check
- writing punishment lines automatically
- how to print the text.

ISBN 1-85365-351-9

PRISMA *be an* expert

also in this series:

Word Processing with Word for Windows

be an expert!

If you have Windows on your computer, there is no better word processing program than Word for Windows. It is clear and easy to operate. But how do you learn the basic skills? If you use this book, you can find out how to apply many word processing features: you can create text in columns just as in newspapers and magazines, use various types of letters and signs, even place drawings in your documents and letters, and much more.

It does not matter if you have not worked with this program before - everything is explained in detail right from the very beginning. When you have worked through this book, the quality of your letters and documents will surprise your friends, parents and teachers!

Some of the exercises in this book:

- making an invitation to a party
- changing the appearance of letters (large, small, bold, underlined, italics, spacing etc.)
- how to print the text
- using the automatic spelling check
- writing a 'real' letter.

ISBN 1-85365-341-1

PRISMA be an expert

also in this series:

Designing with CorelDRAW

be an expert!

CorelDRAW is an all-round graphic program. Even if you cannot draw, that is no handicap whatsoever! You can use CorelDRAW for all kinds of jobs such as creating the drawing itself, adjusting it and colouring and recolouring. But you can also go much further: you can apply 3D effects to your drawings, make them larger or smaller, manipulate parts of them and have drawings flow into one another. In addition, you can make your own logos and letter headings, calendars, diagrams and posters. This book deals with many of these topics and more, and it provides numerous tips to get the best results from any graphic idea.

It does not matter if you have never worked with this program before. This book provides a step-by-step guide right from the beginning. If you are at all interested in drawing, comics or computer art, this book is for you!

ISBN 1-85365-356-X

PRISMA

be an expert

also in this series:

Calculating with Lotus 1-2-3

be an expert!

Everybody wants to use Lotus 1-2-3 to make calculations. But... how do you go about it? If you use this book, you will find out exactly how to let Lotus 1-2-3 do the work, such as adding up numbers, calculating averages, sorting information into the order you want, making diagrams and charts etc. It doesn't matter if you have never worked with this program before, everything is explained right from the beginning.

When you have finished this book, you will be able to make attractive pages of almost everything involving numbers: pocket money, school report cards, goals for and against, athletics or swimming times, beats per minute, you name it!

This book includes:

- checking income and expenditure so that you know where all your pocket money goes
- calculating averages so that you can work out your examination results
- making diagrams so that comparisons can be understood in one glimpse

Give your pocket calculator to somebody as a birthday present. If you have Lotus 1-2-3 you will no longer need it!

ISBN 1-85365-361-6

PRISMA *be an* expert

also in this series:

Working with DOS and Windows
be an expert!

Before you can do anything with the computer, you must know how to work with DOS and Windows. These are the programs you need to start up other programs (a graphic program, a word processor, a calculating program and so on).

In the DOS section, you will learn how to do the most common jobs when working with the computer: copying files and disks, looking to see what is on a diskette, starting up programs, getting rid of files etc.

You will need Windows to work with some programs. This program has a very good graphic screen in which you can carry out all kinds of jobs. You can run several programs at one time in Windows. The different programs are then displayed in separate windows.

You will also learn to work with the most important applications provided by Windows: drawing pictures using Paintbrush, writing letters using Write, working with the Calculator.

When you have finished this book, you will be a skilled computer user and you will be able to get to grips with any computer program!

ISBN 1-85365-302-0